William Logan Fisher

An Inquiry Into the Laws of Organized Societies

As Applied to the Alleged Decline of the Society of Friends

William Logan Fisher

An Inquiry Into the Laws of Organized Societies
As Applied to the Alleged Decline of the Society of Friends

ISBN/EAN: 9783743441705

Manufactured in Europe, USA, Canada, Australia, Japa

Cover: Foto ©Suzi / pixelio.de

Manufactured and distributed by brebook publishing software
(www.brebook.com)

William Logan Fisher

An Inquiry Into the Laws of Organized Societies

AN INQUIRY

INTO THE

LAWS OF ORGANIZED SOCIETIES,

AS APPLIED

TO THE ALLEGED DECLINE

OF

THE SOCIETY OF FRIENDS.

BY

WILLIAM LOGAN FISHER.

PUBLISHED BY T. ELLWOOD ZELL.

1860.

[The following advertisement appeared in " The Friend,"
published in London.]

SOCIETY OF FRIENDS.

PRIZE ESSAY.

A GENTLEMAN who laments that notwithstanding the population of the United Kingdom has more than doubled itself in
the last fifty years, the Society of Friends is less in number
than at the beginning of the century; and who believes that
the Society at one time bore a powerful witness to the world
concerning some of the errors to which it is most prone, and
some of the truths which are the most necessary to it; and
that this witness has been gradually becoming more and more
feeble, is anxious to obtain light respecting the causes of this
change. He offers a Prize of ONE HUNDRED GUINEAS for the
best Essay that shall be written on the subject, and a Prize of
FIFTY GUINEAS for the one next in merit. He has asked three
gentlemen, not members of the Society of Friends, to pronounce
judgment on the Essays which shall be sent to them. They
have all some acquaintance with the history of the Society,
and some interest in its existing members; and as they are
likely to regard the subject from different points of view, he
trusts that their decision will be impartial; that they will not
expect to find their own opinions represented in the Essays;
and that they will choose the one which exhibits most thought
and Christian earnestness, whether it is favorable or unfavor-
able to the Society, whether it refers the diminution of its influence to degeneracy, to something wrong in the original
constitution of the body, to the rules which it has adopted for
its government, or to any extraneous cause.

Rev. F. D. Maurice, Chaplain of Lincoln's Inn; Professor
J. P. Nicholl, Glasgow; and Rev. E. S. Pryce, Gravesend,
have agreed to act as adjudicators, to whom the Essays may
be sent, postage free, to the care of C. S. King, Esq., Messrs.
Smith & Elder, Cornhill, on or before 1st October, 1858.
Each Essay to be accompanied by a sealed letter, containing
the name and address of the writer, the Essay and letters to
bear the same motto. The MSS. of the unsuccessful Essays
will be returned on application, with their letters unopened,
and the successful Essays become the property of the donor.

PREFACE.

THE following was prepared in reference to the prize offered for the best Essay on the decline of the Society of Friends in Great Britain and Ireland; others being preferred, it became of course one of the rejected addresses, and as such is now printed.

I have examined the two Essays which received the first and second prize; the first, by John S. Rowntree, is entitled to respectful consideration, from the clear perception he has of the injurious influence of the Quaker discipline; the second, by Thomas Hancock, is marked by much pedantry and learned ignorance. The people of this country, at least, have too much common sense to believe that reformed Romanism or Puseyism affords a relief to the decaying members of the

1*

Society of Friends; and with the reviewer in "The British Friend," I feel equal astonishment that a prize of one hundred guineas should have been awarded to such a production.

I have also read an American view of the causes which have led to the decline of Friends in Great Britain. The points which the author has endeavored to prove as the cause of the decline, appear to have no reference to the Society in this country; indeed, he seems to doubt whether the Society has declined in America.

As neither of these Essays meet my views, I have concluded to print a few copies of my own. I make no apology for it, but unite entirely with the motto of William Penn: "Truth never lost ground by inquiry, because she is most of all reasonable."

My observations apply to no particular class, but are equally applicable to all the divisions of Friends in Great Britain and America. All who have partaken in the errors whence this decline has resulted, are accountable for it.

ESSAY

THE DECLINE OF THE SOCIETY OF FRIENDS.

THE examination of this subject would be mate-
rially aided if we could decide beforehand what
constitutes Quakerism. What is the creed of the
Society of Friends? what is the standard by which
it is to be judged? what its constitution or elementary law? Without understanding this, we are
liable to receive for facts what are not facts, and
to go blindly on an uncertain path.

It is asserted that the Society has a creed, and
we are referred for its discovery to the early
Quaker books. These are of uncertain tenor, and
are liable to almost any construction which we may
be inclined to place upon them. There is none to
interpret; and an examination, instead of making
the subject clearer, only makes it more confused.

There are some general principles existing, in

their own nature, of universal application, and to these it is needful to advert as connected with the subject, before we examine its creed.

No serious mind will doubt that there is a universal harmony throughout creation. In the material world, it is manifested as perfectly in the dewdrop, on the spear of grass, as in the heavens.

> "That very law that moulds a tear,
> And bids it trickle from its source,
> That law preserves the earth a sphere,
> And guides the planets in their course."

In man's physical frame, perfect health is the natural result of the harmonious action of each individual part, and we have reason to know that this extends to the minutest insect that crawls on the ground. Thus also it is with all those contrivances which man makes to increase his comfort and promote his aims in life. From the spinning-wheel which the thrifty housewife turns with her foot to the elaborated steam-engine, all their respective parts must harmonize and be adapted to the power and strength of the machine. The pitch of every wheel must correspond to its fellow, or its effect will be destroyed, and the end in view defeated.

The mechanic who applies his square and compass to the formation of his building, may little suspect that they point to principles whose source

is in the Eternal mind, and without an adherence
thereto his building would fall to the ground.

Let us not suppose that this harmony extends
only to material things; that it is one thing in
physics another in morals; one thing in the government of a State, another in the government of a
religious society: each has a harmony consistent
with its peculiar organization, but all connected by
a universal harmony, the source and centre of
which is the Divine mind. A comprehension of
this truth would save trouble and prevent subsequent difficulty in attempts to form associations in
human society. In general, without understanding
this principle, it is practically observed, or there
would be discord throughout the world.

It is evident that association is consistent with
the Divine harmony. All creatures congregate for
the proper accomplishment of those ends for which
they are created. Associations seem to be equally
consistent with the nature of man. We find them
among the simple children of the forest: the Indians of America have their chiefs, the wandering
Arabs of the desert have their sheiks, each governing an organization consistent with their rude state.
These things, so universal and enduring, are not
the effect of chance. Religious societies, formed
within organized governments, are but wheels
within wheels. One law extends to all alike, and
they will only be competent to the end for which
they were instituted, as each part is adapted to

every other part, forming one general harmony. These are unchangeable principles, applicable alike to every organized society among men, whether religious, political, benevolent, financial, or domestic. Though differing in their objects, they are all alike governments, subject to the same general laws, and every deviation from their appointed harmony is to be atoned for by suffering. The Society of Friends forms no exception to this universal law.

We may draw some striking illustrations from civil government. Long-continued infringements of the rights of man, produced in France that most memorable revolution, which, for successive years, deluged the streets of the principal cities with blood. England has not been exempt from her own troubles. A want of harmony in the respective parts, has again and again, brought the government to the verge of ruin. No reflecting mind that carefully considers the nature of these two governments, for the last hundred years, can fail to perceive how greatly they have strengthened themselves, how much more united the people are, as the contradictions, which were incorporated into their systems have been done away. The American Revolution, which so signally checked the power of the Crown, apparently saved the mother country from a more violent convulsion at home. At the period of the outlawry of Wilkes, and the riots of Lord George Gordon, the government of Great

Britain had comparatively no power. She was afraid to trust her army for the preservation of peace, because of the manifest contradictions in the government, and infringement of the rights of the people. The proper object of all government, is to promote the comfort and well-being of the governed;—whenever it is diverted to sinister purposes, mercenary armies become needful, as engines to its power. A careful examination of the principles upon which associations are held together, will be a certain guide in indicating their result.

The United States forms an illustration of the truth of this argument. The general features of the government are harmonious, yet there are two disturbing elements, which are producing their inevitable effect. First, there are two sovereign powers in each individual State: the precise limits of each has never yet been defined:—hence conflict. Secondly, there is human slavery, which cannot be made to harmonize with the elementary principles of a free government, and the inevitable effect is discord.

The Quaker colony of Pennsylvania was founded by men of great private worth, the governor, the magistrates, the legislators were all Quakers. It was one of the most peaceable governments that ever existed. Yet it was not altogether so, because, combined with the free government, was a feudal lord, an hereditary governor, not amenable to the people, and this contradiction was a source of unnumbered difficulties.

The world can scarcely furnish a more impressive lesson, than is to be found in the history of the Society of Friends. They assume to be a peaceable society, yet no organization can be peaceable, unless its foundations are laid in harmonious principles. Many of the individuals of the Society are elevated and pure ; there are no better people ; none more ardently desiring peace and concord, yet as an organized body, they cannot preserve peace. Exposition of their principles has followed exposition, advices without number, line upon line and precept upon precept, yet instead of strength, they have had weakness, instead of peace and harmony, schism and discord. These results they cannot change, but by removing the causes from which they spring ; they are the inevitable effects of the inharmonious nature of the organization.

This will be apparent when we advert to the fact, that in the schisms that have taken place, the wisest and best have most actively participated : thus manifesting this great truth, that the more earnest the efforts to carry into effect the contradictions of an imperfect system, the more apparent will be the discord resulting therefrom.

The decline in the Society is often attributed to an increase of individual wealth, to birthright membership, and to a want of individual faithfulness.

Each of these may have had its effect, but they are inadequate to account for the decline. The

individual members of the Society of Friends may
be assumed to be, at least, equal in general intelligence, in virtue, and religious experience, to
the members of other religious denominations, yet
while these increase, the numbers in the Society
decline.

Individual wealth is in many cases the natural
effect of that moderation and economy, which form
one of the characteristics of the Society. If it is
the evil, which it is sometimes supposed to be,
then the Society may be said to carry in its own
bosom the seeds of its dissolution. But it is not so.
Wealth, properly used, is much more likely to increase, than to decrease the numbers in the Society,
and a judicious expenditure of money, wherever
money is in excess, is a good, and not an evil;
a virtue, not a vice.

None of these things are sufficient to account
for the decline, and yet the cause seems sufficiently
apparent. The founders of the Society appear to
have been unaware of those safeguards that are
essential to the well-being of every organized body,
and the result was inevitable. That degree of
peace that has attended the Society is to be attributed to individual excellence, and not to its system. In their early days, Friends seem to have
had no idea of establishing a separate society.
The organization appears to have been a work of
necessity, having in view the praiseworthy object
of assisting those who were suffering.

When the English Friends aided William Penn
in forming a constitution and laws for his colony,
they manifested the most expanded views of the
rights of man. Every safeguard was provided to
check the encroachments of power. His constitution insured peace, and was the admiration of the
world. When the same Friends formed a constitution for the Quaker society, these safeguards
were all forgotten, and the inevitable result was
discord and decline. William Penn says in his
Preface to the Laws of Pennsylvania: "Any
government is free to the people under it, where
the laws rule, and the people are a party to those
laws; and more than this is tyranny, oligarchy, or
confusion."

In Friends' Society the people never were a
party to its laws; it has been ruled by an oligarchy
from the first,—a favored few, who believed that
they had a Divine right to rule, and that it was
the duty of the mass to render obedience.

There are four primary principles needful for
every organization among men:

First. That it should be harmonious in all its
parts.

Second. That it should be adapted to the wants
and character of the people.

Third. That it should have a clearly-defined
sovereign power, to whom an ultimate appeal should
be made.

Fourth. That the rights of the governed should not be impaired.

Now I undertake to say, serious as the charge is, that each one of these principles has been violated in the organization of the Society of Friends, and that this has been the source of all its difficulties, and of its decline.

First. The discipline of the Society will be found to be inconsistent with its elementary principles.

Second. It is not adapted to the wants and character of its members.

Third. It has no well-defined sovereign power.

Fourth. The rights of the governed, as held out in the elementary principles, have been continually encroached upon.

It is important to this inquiry that we should first ascertain what were the real organic principles of the Society of Friends. It is not too much to say that unless they are strictly analyzed and separated into their respective parts, they can never be understood. The whole catalogue of theological literature can scarcely furnish a more contradictory, confused mass of elementary principles, than have been put forth by the Society from the days of George Fox to the present time. They shifted their ground so much that they were often accused, in the early days, of having changed their principles. This they denied, and appeared to prove it to their own satisfaction.

I am bound to say, because it is the truth, that there was a great want of simplicity and of plainness of language among the early Friends, upon the subject of their doctrines, and this exists to the present day. They shelter themselves under texts of Scripture, which are ambiguous and admit of two interpretations; and there is hardly a point of their faith which is plainly and explicitly set forth.

The Society had its foundation in the most beautiful elementary principle that has ever engaged the attention of man; a principle claimed to have existed from the foundation of the world, and to correspond with the feelings of the wisest and best of every age and country. That principle is thus explained by themselves:

"Observe," they say, "the difference between the religion which God has taught us and led us into, and the religion of all men upon earth besides. Their religion stands in a scriptural relation, but our religion stands in a principle wherein the Spirit of Light appeareth, where we hear the voice and see the express image of the Heavenly One, even God himself: and we know things not from an outward relation, but from their inward nature, virtue and power."

"Yea! here we must profess we so know things, that we are fully satisfied about them, and could not doubt concerning them, though there had never been a word of Scripture wrote."—(Address to the Royal Society.)

Pennington, one of the most spiritual of the early Quakers, in almost the same words, thus writes : " Our religion stands wholly *out* of that, which all their religion stands *in*. Their religion stands in the Comprehension, in a belief of a literal Relation or Description. Our religion stands in a Principle, which changeth the Mind, wherein the Spirit of Life appeareth to, and witnesseth in the Conscience to, and concerning the things of the Kingdom ; where we hear the Voice, and see the express Image of the Invisible One, and know things not from an outward Relation, but from their inward Nature, Virtue, and Power. Yea, here (we must profess) we so know things, that we are fully satisfied about them, and could not doubt concerning them, though there had never been Word or Letter written of them."—(Pennington's Works, 2d part, p. 54.)

In these words, " Our religion stands in a principle which changeth the mind," the primitive Friends had the most simple organic law, and the most beautiful creed ever dispensed to any religious society. It embraced all that was true, philosophical, and harmonious. What was not of this, was not true Quakerism.

An implicit faith in the Scriptures, is derogatory to the human character. Many of the eminent dignitaries of the Episcopal Church, as Drs. Tillotson and Stillingfleet, and many others quoted by Penn, wholly rejected this idea, placing the in-

2*

terpretation in right reason, and in an enlightened criticism; and this equally applied to every idea presented to the mind, through either written or oral communications. Penn also quotes Cicero in confirmation.—(Penn, 2d vol. pages 344 and 345.)

George Fox was explicit upon this subject: when the Jurist at Nottingham said "it was by the Scriptures men were to try doctrines, religions, and opinions," George Fox interrupting him, exclaimed, " Oh, no! it is not the Scriptures, but it is the Holy Spirit, by which the holy men of old gave forth the Scriptures, whereby religions, opinions, and doctrines, are to be tried."—(Fox's Journal, page 9, &c.)

Fox again says : " Though I read the Scriptures that spake of Christ and God, yet I knew him not but by revelation, as he that had the key did open."

Samuel Fisher, the most eminent biblical scholar that ever appeared in the Society, wrote several hundred folio pages, principally to prove the corruptions and barbarisms, the innumerable faults and errors " of the various readings of the Scriptures," and William Penn, and other eminent Friends, ·published testimonials in favor of his work.*

These may be assumed to be the first doctrines of the Society.

---

* See Samuel Fisher's Testimony.

It was not the establishment of Christianity, as the religion of a sect which they sought, but the Christian religion in its Divine Spirit and essence, which made man a brother to his fellow man throughout the world; not the religion of the Bible, as explained by learned men, but the religion that existed before any Bible was written. A religion whose power was in the convictions of individual minds, and not in any external thing. Howgil on Borroughs* uses this language : "When it pleased the Lord to raise up unto us the ancient horn of salvation, we entered into no external covenant, but trod down under our feet all questioning, debating, reasoning, and contending about religion." This was Quakerism in the day of its power, when it seemed as if all men would become Quakers. This is true Quakerism now, tempered by common sense, the most valuable of all sense, by enlightened reason, the most valuable of all the powers of the mind, and best calculated to restrain that fanaticism, which has so often led men astray.

The London Discipline says : " The foundation on which a true Christian is built, is the Spirit of Christ. Let this, therefore, direct you in all things, both respecting your private conversation, and whatever you do for God in his Church."

The leading feature of this ancient Quakerism as portrayed in these extracts, is, that it rested

* See Howgil's Testimony of Borroughs.

upon man's internal convictions, independent of
the Scriptures, and thus, there was a clear line of
distinction drawn between it and all other professions of religion. "Their religion stands in a
scriptural relation, ours in a principle that changeth
the mind."

The important truths that were uttered by the
early Quakers, before they became strictly an organized body, though sometimes crude and often
rough in the exterior, are among the most remarkable points in their history, whether upon the subject of civil government, or of the duties men owe to
each other. On what might be called deep metaphy-
sics, they were greatly in advance of their age, for
this obvious reason, that they learned the nature
of man from the only true source where that nature could be properly studied, from the internal
operations of their own souls. It would be a reflection upon the common sense of society, to
undertake to prove the truth of this internal evidence;—of this spiritual communion : without it
civil society would be dissolved, and the world
would come to an end.

It is an unchangeable law of our being that all
visible things come by observation. By the eye
we know that a house is a house, and a tree, a tree.
By the ear we can understand that there are lands
and oceans which our eye has never seen ; but invisible things are only known by the intuitive perceptions of our own souls. It is thus, that we

have the knowledge of our own existence. It is by this means alone that purely intellectual subjects are understood. Let us give this intellectual perception what name we may, the moral sense, enlightened reason, the impress of the Divinity, the light of Christ in the soul, it changes in no respect its character, and an unshaken belief in this great idea, formed the foundation on which the early Quakers professed to rest.

In confirmation of the universality of this principle, William Penn quotes from nearly four hundred different authors, many of them the most eminent of the Greeks and Romans, to prove their recognition of the Quaker sentiment; and Barclay half as many more. They and other early Friends, left abundant testimony of their belief, that Quakerism would overspread the world. Edward Borroughs, one of the most eminent among them, used this emphatic language : " We shall be a people when the Egyptians be dead upon the sea-shore, and when the raging sea is dried up. My confidence is sure, that the work of the Lord will prosper, and our testimony shall be glorious forever, and this people shall never be extinguished from being a people." Again he says : " David, Moses, and Jeremiah, and many more testified of in Scripture, were of the same faith with us, the same doctrine and principles; they were Quakers, as their own writings make manifest."—(Borroughs's Works, page 165.)

These were the enlarged views of the early
Friends. As defined by them, Quakerism embraced
the wise and good of all ages, the Greeks and
Romans, the Persians and the Syrians, the Jewish warrior and the Jewish prophet, all who were
believers in the eternal light of truth.

It is to be regretted that after proclaiming to
the world a spiritual doctrine so plain and distinct, they entered into the arena of public dispu-
tation, undertook to explain dogmas which admitted
of no explanation, upon which they did not agree
themselves, and which have been the prolific source
of discord in the Christian world. Becoming thus
entangled with the popular theology of the day, there
was scarcely any intermission of the disputes and
altercations that ensued. Public discussions were
held, where thousands of persons were collected,
which sometimes lasted for successive days, and
proved most disastrous to the peace of the Society.
That simple element of their faith, the daily per-
formance of individual duty, became mixed up and
overlaid with dogmas, with which it had no connection. Were it needful I might make many
more quotations, showing, to use George Fox's own
words, that " their foundation was not on Matthew,
Mark, Luke, and John, but on the internal evidence
of truth in their own minds."—(" News out of the
North," p. 5.)

I shall now present another phase of Quakerism.
The persecutions to which Friends were constantly

exposed, led them to construe their peculiar opinions more and more in accordance with the popular views of the day. One of the most remarkable instances of this was, after denying the supremacy of the Scriptures to consent to make them a test of their doctrines, thus yielding all their argument to their opponents, and relinquishing one of the most important points in primitive Quakerism.

A knowledge of the historic facts on this subject should prove an olive branch of peace to the present Society; for while all parties refer to the ancient writings of Friends, they may find authority there for the most ultra sentiments that have ever been advanced.

Samuel Fuller thus writes: " We believe the Holy Scriptures contain a clear testimony of all – the essentials of the Christian faith; that they are the only fit judge of controversy among Christians; that whatever doctrine is contrary unto their testimony, may therefore be justly rejected as false; and that whatsoever any do, pretending to the Spirit, which is contrary to the Scriptures, ought to be accounted a delusion of the devil."—(See Evans's Exposition.)

Some modern English Quakers go even further than this. In "Portable Evidences of Christianity," Joseph John Gurney says: "The Bible alone fully reveals the nature and character of sin." "It is in the Scriptures only, that the attributes of our Heavenly Father are fully made known to us, and they speak also of the written revelation of God."

According to the original doctrine of Friends, revelation applied to spiritual things, must be spiritual; and though this truth was promulgated by unlearned men, and is contradicted by sectarians, who speak of written revelation applied to the Scriptures, yet no truth, we think, can be more self-evident to a strictly attentive mind than this, as I have said in a former page, that we learn outward things by our outward senses, and spiritual things by the intuitive perceptions in the soul, which no man can obscure or shut out.

Whenever Friends admitted the idea of a written revelation as authoritative, they denied their first principles, and the attempt to reconcile the two has been productive of the utmost confusion and contradiction, and has led into innumerable minor inconsistencies. Vain efforts have been made without number, to reconcile particular passages with preconceived opinions, and it may be doubted whether in a century, one single passage of doubtful meaning has been satisfactorily settled.

The writings of the early Quakers are deemed to be of paramount authority, and yet it is impossible to form from them any correct opinion of what is really the creed, or organic law of the Society, upon the subject of the Scriptures.

Edward Borroughs says : " That is no command of God to me, which he commands to another ;

neither did any of the saints, which we read of in the Scriptures, act by the command which was to another, not having the command to themselves. I challenge to find an example."—(Borroughs's Works, page 47.)

William Penn in opposition to this says: "It is a root of ranterism to assert that nothing is a duty incumbent upon thee, but what thou art persuaded is thy duty."—(Penn's Works, 2d vol. page 69.)

These men may be deemed of equal authority. There are like contradictions upon every other point of doctrine. Upon none are they more apparent, than upon that which is called the doctrine of Christ.

The word Christ as contained in the early books, sometimes means the Spirit of God in the heart, sometimes the outward man Christ, and there is a blending of ideas, contradictory in their nature, from which, with equally apparent reason, different inferences have been drawn by different minds, to suit their preconceived opinions.

The schism that originated with George Keith, that of William Rathbone and the Friends in Ireland, and that of Elias Hicks in America, all had their origin in this source, and in almost every meeting, from the early days of the Society to the present time, disputes upon this subject have had a deleterious influence.

William Penn in his address to Protestants, asks

"What is Christ but Meekness, Justice, Mercy, Patience, and Virtue in perfection?" Thus dropping all reference to the outward manifestation, and adhering to the vital principle or spirit.

It seems to have been an unsettled question with Penn and the early Quakers, whether the manhood was a part of Christ. After much contention in a dispute with the Baptists (mentioned by Clarkson in his Life of Penn, 2d vol. page 98), Penn declared that Christ was not to be divided into parts. Friends were closely pressed for an answer. Penn says: "If we had answered no, we would have been lost. If by Scripture, it would have been not very satisfactory, because they would have asked our understanding of the Scripture." And after much discussion, to the great discomfiture of Penn, Friends declared that the manhood was a part of Christ.

Job Scott, one of the eminent writers on this subject, and believed to be a man of deep religious experience, uses this language: "If I knew Christ no otherwise than they (the professors) teach, describe, and declare him, I think I must be either a sceptic or a deist. I can never see the connection between the sufferings of a body of flesh seventeen or eighteen hundred years ago, and the salvation of an immortal soul at this day. I think the systems by some promulgated for the Gospel of salvation by Jesus, as full fraught with absurdity as

almost anything I have met with in Mahome-
tanism or in the ancient mythology of the
heathen." Elsewhere he says: "I would as soon
trust my immortal state in the profession of deism,
as upon the common notion of salvation by Christ."
(See Salvation by Christ, by Job Scott.)

In contradiction to this, other writers of equal
authority say:—" Christ is the only wise God;
our Saviour, King of kings, and Lord of lords.
That he has washed us from our sins in his own
blood; that he now sitteth on the right hand of
God the Father, in a glorified body, our mediator,
advocate, and intercessor with the Father." These
sentiments and many others connected with the
Atonement, may be found in "Evans's Exposition," from page 59 to 246—to quote them would
transcend the limits of this work. They are sufficient to account for the evil effects that have
flowed from the attempts to compel a uniformity,
as respects this particular doctrine.

In the work referred to, there are twenty pages
devoted to show how fully the early Friends believed in what they considered to be the essential
principle of the Trinity. "We own,'; they say,
"the three that bear record in heaven,—the
Father, the Word, and the Holy Ghost; and these
three are one." They objected to the word Trinity,
because it was not found in the Bible, but held to
the substance. Modern critics have proved this
to be a spurious text.

Of one hundred and thirteen Greek manuscripts
now extant, containing the epistle in which this
text occurs, it is only to be found in one copy. It
is wanting in all the ancient versions of the Vul-
gate; it is not in any Latin copies previous to the
tenth century; it is wanting in Erasmus's edition,
also in that of Luther, and appears to be univer-
sally considered by all biblical critics of the present day, even by Trinitarians, as an interpolation
made for corrupt sectarian purposes.

A modern Quaker uses this language: " Behold
the glorious partner of the Father's throne fully
opening his bosom to the vials of his wrath, groan-
ing and bleeding on the cross in the nature of
man, and bearing in his own body on the tree, the
penalty of the sins of mankind." Again: "Let
us call to mind that, in that hour of unutterable
desertion, the righteous vengeance of God against
a guilty world, was poured forth upon the innocent
substitute."—(Gurney's Treatise on Love to God.)

On the subject of the ministry, George Fox says:

" Let him be Jew or Papist, or Turk or Heathen,
or Protestant, or what sort soever, or such as worship sun or moon, or sticks or stones, let them
have liberty where every one can bring forth his
strength, and have free liberty to speak forth his
mind and judgment."—(See Fox's Doctrines, page
234.)

In direct opposition to this, Barclay, quoting
Titus, says: "Men's mouths must be stopped, or

what blasphemy so horrid, what heresy so damnable, what doctrine of devils, but might harbor itself in the Church of Christ." These conflicting opinions led, as a necessary consequence, to the formation of a discipline by which to establish what was right, and reprove what was wrong, a code of laws by which the Society should be governed. All this produced much contention, and was protested against by many eminent Friends. "We deny not," they say, "the body of people called Quakers, nor as they act in the light, that they have true judgment; but we complain against your Foxonian unity, which consists of certain ministers and elders, which lift up George Fox for a bishop, a pope, and a king, making his papers edicts, and then entitling them the judgment of the body; whereas, indeed, it is but the minds of the cabals of Foxonians; the leaders are the men we strike at."—(See Spirit of the Hat, page 11· to 16.)

Friends had been goaded almost to desperation by the persecutions which had been heaped upon them. Church and State conspired against them. They were committed to loathsome jails;—at one period there were more than four thousand of them in prison, where many perished. Yet here was an enemy greater than them all,—bitter and unrelenting dissensions among themselves: the natural effect of departing from their own simple doctrine.

This is believed to have been the most critical time that ever occurred in the Society. The supre-

macy of the principle of truth in the mind,—liberty
of conscience,—individual faithfulness to manifested
duty, were all ignored to introduce another element,
which was the supremacy of the Quaker Discipline.
Fox was the active agent in the work of trampling
under foot principles he held in the beginning. In
this he was seconded by Barclay, Penn, and many
of the leading members, yet there was a strong and
powerful party in opposition. It was a period of great
excitement in the British empire, and the Society
of Friends was surrounded by difficulties. Many
odd people appeared, among the most extravagant
of whom were the Anabaptists of Munster. Friends
were accused of a complicity with Ranters, Fifth
Monarchy men, Deists, and others. If the government and the clergy were equally their enemies,
the early Quakers were not behindhand in their
controversy with them. They opposed them all
with unsparing language,—uttering prophecies
against the Church, the priests, and the State, few
of which have ever been fulfilled. This period of
British history is technically called the reign of
the Saints. William Penn thus characterized it:
" Oh, the unheard of hypocrisy of that age!
Sycophants in grain, enough to poison the whole
world with their flatteries, whose interest was their
conscience, and power their religion, devotion only
serving to stalk their stratagems to promotion; but
the just God has swept them off the stage, and their

sun is set, and shall never rise more."—(Penn's
Works, 2d vol. page 86.)

It was at this unhappy period that the Society
was formed, and we need not be surprised that it
became inextricably entangled in the sectarianism
of the day. After pleading for liberty of conscience, it limited it so as effectually to deny it.
Both Robert Barclay and William Penn took up
their pens to espouse the cause of Church government. Barclay produced that remarkable work
called "The Anarchy of the Ranters." Many eminent men sustained it, and decided that the " sanctified members of the Society," being the " Church
of Christ," had the power of determining all dis-
puted questions, that " such shall be bound in
heaven whom they bind on earth, and such loosed
in heaven whom they loose on earth." This is
the language of Barclay; it was the establishment
of a sovereign power with which the mass of the
members had no connection, and of a character
which is believed to have been false in principle.

This book begins with an assumption on the title
page, that the ancient Apostolic order of the
Church of Christ, and the pure principles of the
Gospel, are restored by the Quakers; but I am inclined to believe, that its details are inconsistent
with the avowed principles of the Society.

It produced much discord at the time of its pub-
lication. Barclay was called upon to vindicate
himself, and many Friends were mixed up with

the dispute. A natural result was the establishment of superior orders of men (sanctified members, as Barclay calls them). Meetings were organized like wheels within wheels: Meetings of Ministers and Elders, Meetings of Overseers, 2d day Morning Meetings, each having a distinct authority, and constituting an organization of its own. In addition to these, there was a Meeting for Sufferings, that represented and exercised the powers of the Yearly Meeting, when that body was no longer in session; all these were secret societies, the members of which were able by their influence, to suppress all sentiments different from their own, and thus to control the Society. In this way, an oligarchy was formed in reality, though not in name, which took away the rights of the members, by a power created by themselves, and which was in direct violation of the first principles of the Society.

Can any serious mind believe that all this complicated machinery was needful to carry out those simple views promulgated by the early Quakers? Perfect individualism, or independence, is inconsistent with our present state of existence. Religious organizations are the effect of our sympathies and affinities, and though not absolutely needful to a virtuous and religious life, yet they suit the constitution of many minds, and when formed, should be consistent and harmonious in all their parts. Here in the Society of Friends, was the

most simple and beautiful organic law, combined,
perhaps, with the most complicated discipline,—the
most confused doctrines that the world can furnish.
In Barclay's work, he compares this plan of
submitting all questions to the " sanctified members," with that of the Romanists, and the gene-
rality of the Protestants, and he asks that they
should be seriously examined. The history of
nearly two hundred years demonstrates, that the
Quaker plan of deciding contested questions, is
inferior to them all. There is no power on earth,
that can determine who are the " sanctified members," and hence, according to the early Friends,
who have the right to judge.

I have before stated that all organizations among
men are subject to the same general laws ; now let
us listen to the unquestionable truths of history.
In these United States there are upwards of thirty
individual commonwealths. The questions that
come before them, many of which are deeply interesting to the welfare of society, are settled by
the simple expression of the sentiments of the
people,—by that system of voting that Barclay
so much reprobates. Now, if this plan had been
adopted among Friends, modified by existing circumstances in such a manner that the unbiassed
sentiment of every member who had arrived at
majority, could have been given either in person,
or by representatives honestly chosen, no reasonable doubt can exist that it would in great measure

have prevented those schisms which have distracted the Society, and been a prolific cause of its decline. It would have given to each individual a direct interest in its welfare, and a consequent responsibility. In less than thirty years after the formation of the Discipline, three important schisms occurred. They were somewhat different in their causes, but all arising from what were believed to be improper interference with the rights of the people. The name of John Perott is identified with the first. The charges against him were :

First. That he wore his beard.

Second. That he did not rise on his feet (and take off his hat) at the time of public prayer.

Third. That he manifested an ostentatious disposition by signing some of his letters John, without Perott.

In the records of ecclesiastical history, few more absurd cases than this can be found.

When it is remembered, that the Society claimed great liberty of conscience to itself, and that the very basis of its organic law was the right of private judgment, can there remain a reasonable doubt that there was, in this case, a violation of the principles which had been proclaimed by the Society? Of what consequence was it whether John Perott wore his hat or his beard? why should not men be at liberty to sit or stand or even to kneel down, as is often done at a time of public prayer? Why should a society be shocked at a

little extravagance in a man for omitting his sur-
name to an epistle, when the leaders were commit-
ting ten times as much extravagance in other ways?

The second schism took place long before the
first had subsided. Wilkinson and Story, William
Rogers, an eminent merchant of Bristol, Thomas
Crisp, and Charles Harris, most of them eminent
preachers, were the prominent men in this schism.
The cause was a decided opposition to the Discipline; they alleging that the Society had got along
heretofore peaceably without a discipline, and that
it was altogether unnecessary; and they particularly objected to the separate organization of
women's meetings, and to the inquisitorial nature
of the queries. The oligarchy condemned them as
aspiring men, and disowned them.

The third schism was that of George Keith. It
began in Pennsylvania, and was of a doctrinal
character. He conceived the idea that some of
the eminent Friends in Pennsylvania entertained
Socinian sentiments. He was joined by some distinguished men in the Province, and various separate
meetings were established. The case was referred
to London, where he was condemned, and he finally
joined the Established Church, and became a bitter
opponent of the Society.

I have examined with care Keith's narrative, as
well as those published by the Society, and have
no doubt that both this schism and those that pre-
ceded it would have been avoided or arrested, had

the authority of the body rested, not with the
" sanctified members," but with the people themselves.

The evil which has resulted from the rule of this
oligarchy, has not been negative only; it has been
attended by positive evils, which, in their consequences, have done more than all besides, to bring
the Society to its present weak state, as a few facts
will demontrate.

In the important schism that occurred about
thirty years ago in Pennsylvania, by an accurate
return from some of the Monthly Meetings, the
proportion of those who were called orthodox to
those of the opposite party, was nearly one-seventh
of the former to six-sevenths of the latter. Another return makes the proportion one-sixth of
the former to five-sixths of the latter; yet this
small minority assumed to be the " true church,"
to use Barclay's expression—the " sanctified members," and actually went through the form of disowning the rest, to all appearance as excellent as
themselves.

At the separation of the Baltimore Yearly
Meeting, while, on one side, there were nine hundred individuals, members of the Society, on the
other there were but seventy-six; yet this small
number claimed, as in the former case, to be the
true Society, and, extraordinary as it may appear,
they testified against all the others and disowned
them : in both cases, men in every respect as worthy

as themselves. The pretended charge was unsoundness of faith. The real difficulty was, that the larger body claimed a right which seemed to be guaranteed to all,—the right of private judgment, in a case involving no moral delinquency, no deviation from what they believed to be the primary principles of the Society, but in which some of the elders assumed the authority to decide.

These may be admitted to be extreme cases, yet they are examples of what has often occurred in a more limited degree where an oligarchy has assumed the right to govern; even admitting, which I do not, that this oligarchy was composed of the best members of the Society; yet such men are naturally conservative; living in an atmosphere created in part by their own excellence, they are not the men for reformation, even where the necessity for reformation exists. Hence it is that laws remain in force which are adverse to the wants and feelings of the age, and the Society becomes petrified in its errors.

One of the natural consequences of the rule of this oligarchy is, that being thus satisfied with things as they are, and controlling, to a considerable extent, the affairs of the Society, they become a barrier to all progress, and Friends, who should be of all others least traditionary, are perhaps the most so.

The writings of early Friends are valuable as showing the opinions of those who have gone be-

4

fore; but the very essence of their doctrine forbids their being considered a standard for succeeding generations. The creed of the Society being unwritten, it is alleged that it is to be drawn from these ancient writings; and, like the Constitution of Great Britain, it is to be found in the precedents of former generations. But the essential element of the British Constitution is that there are courts to interpret it, to adapt it to the progress of time, and the feelings of the age. The Society of Friends have no such courts, no supreme power to explain its creed, and it shelters itself under the ambiguities of the Scriptures; thus increasing the obscurity, and leaving individuals to construe it to suit their own ideas, each having a creed of his own. This is just as it should be, and ought to give no offence; but the sad part of it is, that offence is taken, and the oligarchy claim to dictate what its members shall believe. In the division of 1827, the Friends (called Hicksites) claimed to be the true Society, and their claim was unquestionably correct; yet the Orthodox believed themselves to be equally correct, because the records could be read either way. The effect was that a schism ensued, uncalled for, if men had not undertaken to condemn their fellow-members on points that they did not understand themselves.

It is the part of wisdom for every organization to establish a constitution or a creed, according to

its wants, yet this should be confined to tangible
things, that the members could all understand,
that admitted of no dispute, and it should be harmonious in itself. Then it would insure to the Society all the harmony that an organization could
bestow. To attempt to fix the faith of men is to
assume the powers of the Most High. The Reformation of Luther, while it protested against image
worship, established the idolatry of the Bible, and
from that has grown up many of those dogmas and
frivolous absurdities which have deluged the Christian world with blood.

A belief in the dogmas of the Christian religion,
in the outward atonement, a specified faith in the
offices and mission of Christ, in original sin, in
making the Scripture the supreme arbiter in the
affairs of life, a literal belief in the Mosaic account of the creation, and all the separate questions growing out of these, the primitive Friends,
according to Francis Howgil, as quoted, trampled
under their feet as forming no part of the Christian
religion. Yet in violation of this principle, the
London Yearly Meeting established the following
creed, which I extract from the London Discipline:

"If there be any such gross errors, false doctrines, or mistakes, held by any professing truth,
as are either against the validity of Christ's sufferings, blood, resurrection, ascension, or glory in the
heavens, according as they are set forth in the
Scriptures, or any ways tending to the denial of

the heavenly man Christ, such persons ought to be diligently instructed and admonished by faithful friends, and not to be exposed by any to public reproach ; and where the error proceeds from ignorance and darkness of their understanding, they ought the more meekly and gently to be informed; but if any shall wilfully persist in error in point of faith, after being duly informed, then such to be further dealt with according to Gospel order, that the truth, Church, or body of Christ, may not suffer by any particular pretended member that is so corrupt."—(W. E.)

Properly considered, the creed of the early Friends contained but one idea, which I have already quoted. "Our religion stands in a principle that changes the mind." Every effort that they made to explain this, to reconcile it to Scripture or to the opinions of other men, only seemed to lead them to confusion. They declared that this rested on their own convictions, distinct from the Scriptures; yet, denying their own words, they formed this creed in conformity with the popular doctrines of the day. It was earnestly protested against by many intelligent minds, and never was adopted in America. Friends declared in the meeting in Philadelphia, that they knew but one principle, and that was "the light within." Thomas Fitzwater, a preacher, said in meeting, that he knew no man Christ Jesus in heaven *without him,* but the grace of God within him. William Stockdale, an ancient minister, and others spoke to the same effect.*

This creed may be said to have been absolutely and unequivocally in opposition to the whole spirit and bearing of the early and organic principles of the Society.

The Society also undertook to decide what was the proper construction to be placed on the various texts of Scripture, and if individuals did not conform thereto, they were made offenders.

All these efforts were fruitless. If there was an outward confession of faith, it was without conviction, without producing any real uniformity.

The evidence is too plain to admit of a doubt, that all this was the work of the oligarchy of the "sanctified members." At the division in 1827, three-fourths of the members in the Middle States, constituting the most numerous body of American Friends, practically protested against the attempt to form a creed and to control their judgment. There is no doubt that the opinions of Elias Hicks embraced those ultra doctrines of George Fox and Isaac Pennington to which I have referred, and which are even more direct than those which have been attributed to him; and it is quite certain that the bulk of the members who, it may be said, followed his standard, concerned themselves much less about his particular doctrines, than respecting

* See Works of George Keith.

the attempt to control them. With strict observation, I have never yet found the difference between the mass of Friends who form the two great divisions of the Society in Pennsylvania, neither is there any reason, except their prejudices, why they should not be again united for all good purposes. The division was brought about by the Orthodox party, not among the young and indiscreet, but by the well-meaning and excellent; so far, however, erroneous in their conscientious persuasions, that they believed the welfare of the Society was involved in the necessity of their carrying into effect their own particular notions. Deeply instructive is this schism. All the efforts of the wisest and best in the Society were unable to arrest its progress; for this evident reason, that an attempt was made to carry into effect a system full of inconsistencies; and it may not be irrelevant to the subject of this inquiry (I say it with no unkindness), they have dug a pit and they have fallen into it themselves. They cannot change this result. Their individual excellence may for a time save them from difficulty, but those who do not fulfil the Divine laws must needs in the end change their course or be crushed thereby; and this applies no more to one division of the Society than to another, no more to Friends than to any other people;* but it may serve to explain some of the dreadful conflicts in the so-called Christian world.

* Frederick Foxton, of Stoke Prior, one of the most intelli-

The salutary influence of free discussion through
the press, must be admitted by all; yet this has
been lost to the Society of Friends by means of
a severe and exacting censorship, regarding the
usages, testimonies, and doctrines of the Society,
only equalled by that of Napoleon I, over the
French press, in the days of his power.

So long ago as the schism of Wilkinson and
Story, in the latter part of the seventeenth century,
this censorship prevailed. Rogers, an eminent
merchant of Bristol, wrote an account of his dis-
satisfaction, for which he was required to make an

gent Episcopal ministers in England, speaks thus of the Episcopal Church, showing that the decadence in the Society of
Friends is not peculiar to it: "Her whole head is sick; her
whole heart is faint; even in the multitude of her counsellors,
there is no strength, but rather confusion, vacillation, and dis-
may. In spite of a few spasmodic and convulsive throes, her
days are most assuredly already numbered." Again, he says,
of the ministering clergy, "I require alone that they suffer as
far as possible; that judgment should go by default where
they have no rational plea for the defence of an insignificant
rite or obsolete form. If the Church will not speak the truth,
let her at least be silent. If she will not inform, if she fears to
enlighten the consciences of her hearers, let her at least cease
to mystify and deceive them. The concession I require is far
less than her bigoted supporters are willing to believe, for
her authority is hourly decreasing, and every attempt to restore it but hastens its decline."* Assuredly, this decline in
the Episcopal Church may be traced to the same source as
that in the Society of Friends.

* Foxton on Popular Christianity, pp. 36 and 220.

apology, as was another Friend who printed the work. A third, who sold it, refusing to make any acknowledgment of error, was disowned.

A respectable printer, now living in Philadelphia, was disowned a few years ago for printing a work not containing one word immoral, irreligious, or unkind to any sect or individual, but which, in some parts, had a remote bearing upon the doctrines of the Society. He appealed to the Yearly Meeting against such flagrant injustice, alleging he had done it in the line of his business, and knew nothing of the contents of the work. He appealed in vain.

William Rathbone, of Liverpool, a man of superior intelligence and worth, was disowned for publishing an account of the schism among Friends in Ireland, and this by a society that had published elaborate appeals for liberty of conscience.

William Penn says, " Liberty of conscience is agreeable to the laws of nature, reason, and civil government ; to the example as well as the doctrine of Christ." And he refers to many states, empires, and kingdoms, that were saved by an extension of this liberty.

Barclay and Fox speak extensively in its favor ; yet liberty of conscience seems to have meant a different thing outside of the Society to what it did when applied to its own members.

It is a melancholy truth, yet it is a truth, that no true liberty of conscience has heretofore existed in the Society of Friends. If the extension of this privilege, according to William Penn, saved France, Germany, and Holland, and other states, from ruin, may we not also believe that withholding it has been one cause of the decline of the Society. It is understood, that the censorship over the press has been broken down by its own weight in London ; and, to the credit of that portion of the Society peculiarly called Friends, in opposition to the Orthodox, it may be stated, that they have mostly, if not altogether, abandoned it. If any relics of it remain, it cannot long exist with a free people.

It is the unnecessary denial of those civil rights which seem naturally to belong to all, that has made the Society of Friends so unpopular with those thinking minds who felt that they had a right to judge for themselves. Religious associations that interfere with the first principles of individual duty, are in reality violating what they profess to protect.

Many of the eminent authors of antiquity, whose sentiments are still cherished, rejected associations altogether. They taught in the grove, in the garden, and by the wayside ; and hence have been called " walking philosophers."

In recent times it has been said that it requires a great mind to calculate how much is due to circumstances without detriment to principles. Assuredly there is a point where principles and circumstances may be made to harmonize ; if not, there can be no permanent existence for a religious society. The forms and ceremonies in what is called the Christian world, have no vitality, and are not calculated for intelligent people. Coercion may be needful to prevent man from injuring his fellow-man, but coercion in religious societies is persecution. At present, the Society of Friends is sustained by the excellence of its individual members, which gives it temporary vitality, and enables it partially to surmount the contradictions in its organic laws, its childish peculiarities, and ossified discipline. The Discipline of the Society of Friends is a system of coercion; its provisions are in many respects arbitrary and unworthy the regard of an intelligent people. And this we claim to have been one of the principal causes of the decline of the Society. We desire not to awaken any prejudice, but a calm consideration of the facts before us.

If the object of a religious society is to promote religion, then we deny its right to interfere with the faith of its members, seeing that faith is not at our command; we deny its right to enter into our domicils and interfere with the innocent enjoyment of our children.

The proceedings of the Society in the exercise of its discipline, form a melancholy history of arbitrary power; yet the oligarchy in the Society has always been sufficiently strong to crush every attempt radically to reform it.

That portion of the Society which are peculiarly called Friends, in contradistinction to the Orthodox Friends, have, within the last few years, removed many of the objectionable parts of the Discipline respecting marriage ; thus restoring those civil rights which the laws of the country guarantee to all. Individuals may marry in the meeting-house, or out of it, by Friends' ceremony, without offence, and thus they have strengthened their Society to an extent they hardly know themselves. The development of true civilization has always corresponded with freedom of mind.

Some modification of the Discipline on the subject of marriage has been made by London Yearly Meeting, and by other yearly meetings who correspond with it on this continent.

Till within the past few years, Friends have not been allowed even to be present when one of their members has been married to a person not a member, and in support of this rule, thousands have been disowned. It may not be too much to assume that the descendants of persons permanently separated from the Society by marriage alone, would outnumber all its present members. Many have been disowned for having music in their houses ; for attending other places of worship ; for their dress and address ; not because they were unfaithful to their duties, but because they transgressed some rule of the Discipline.

Though Providence has placed before us the beautiful colors of the rainbow, and clothed the

flowers of the field with every tint that can delight
the eye, it has been deemed by Friends most pleas-
ing in His holy sight to select those hues that He
has the least regarded, while to imitate the war-
bling of the birds, or the soft sound of the Æolian
harp, created also by His power, is considered a
crime, to be visited by the condemnation of the
Society. Thus are the young asked to sacrifice
what they esteem the beautiful, to an artificial and
sectarian taste.

Elizabeth Fry says, "Bitter experience has
proved to me that Friends do rest too much in
externals." * * * "And this has reconciled me
in a measure to so many of my children leaving
them." (Her Life, by her daughter.)

Society is necessarily weakened by making offences where there is no real offence; by enforc-
ing laws to remedy evils, where no real evil exists.

Friends came forth boldly, avowing their separation from all the religions of the day. They appeared before princes and potentates, pleading the
cause of the oppressed, everywhere manifesting
that their power was in the strength of their convictions, and not derived from any outward source,
and their meeting-houses overflowed with members.
They descended to embrace those dogmas which
have been the prolific source of discord in the
Christian world; to consider the color of a ribbon,
and the form of a garment; and their meeting-
houses are comparatively vacant. And the ques-

tion is asked, Why the Society has declined? and "Why that powerful witness to the world concerning some of its errors, has been gradually more and more feeble?"

In summing up the causes of the decline, any degeneracy in the character of its individual members enters not into the question, because, as before stated, their virtue and intelligence are supposed to be at least equal to that of the members of other religious societies which have not declined.

It is not in their individual wealth. It is doubted whether this is greater among them than in the members of other religious societies, and thus it comes not into our view as a particular cause of the decline. If ever they have had greater wealth it is possible that they have had more active benevolence, and here is in part at least a compensation. It is not to be traced to error in their fundamental principle. Far from it. This embraces all that is good in the moral world. The Church of God, in its expanded sense, coëval with humanity, exists in this Divine principle; it gives strength to the civil law, to political affairs, to civil and religious life. It is the conservative principle of humanity; without it, the world would be a desert, and society come to an end. It gives a power to the arts and sciences which nothing else can impart; and, however feeble may be its acknowledgment, and imperfect the regard that is paid to it, apart from bigotry and sectarianism, it is slowly but

5

surely extending its influence throughout the
world. Even some of the members of the Established churches are proclaiming its beauty and
power, with a clearness seldom attained by its own
writers.—(See Foxton on Popular Christianity.)

Bancroft, in his History of the United States,
says : " The principle of the Quakers contained a
moral revolution. If it flattered self-love, it also
established absolute freedom of mind ; trod every
idolatry under foot, and entered the strongest protest against the forms of a hierarchy." Hooker
thus beautifully characterizes this principle, applied to law : " Of law, there can be no less acknowledged, than that her seat is the bosom of God ;
her voice, the harmony of the world. All things
in heaven and on earth do her homage ; the very
least as feeling her care, and the greatest as not
exempted from her power ; both angels, and men,
and creatures of what condition soever, though
each in different sort and manner, yet all with uniform consent admiring her as the mother of peace
and joy."

Ruskin thus speaks of the application of this
principle to the fine arts : " It was only when individual religion entered into all the concerns of
life, giving a serenity of mind and energy to all
their actions, it was then only that the fine arts
flourished in Italy. As this declined, their spirit
dwindled down, and the authors became copyists,
one of another."—(Stories of Venice, page 89.)

Dugald Stewart uses these words respecting its effect on science : " Perhaps it would not be going too far to assert that the principles of natural religion have a relation to almost all the truths we know, in the moral, intellectual, and material worlds." * * * * " It is a strong confirmation of these remarks that the most important discoveries, both in moral and physical science, have been made by men friendly to the principles of natural religion."—(Stewart's Works, 3d vol. p. 464.)

There is no other interpretation to be given to the term " natural religion," than the belief in the sufficiency of the spontaneous conviction of man's own mind. Against every other religion,—the religion of books, and the orthodox religions of the day,—the controversy of early Friends was poured out in almost unmeasured terms.

We have given these extracts from wise and intelligent authors, to show how intimately connected the fundamental principle of Friends is with all that is valuable in the world. In comparison to its promises in its early days, the Society may be considered to have been a melancholy failure. It has fallen far short of what its friends expected from it; yet while it has made no ostentatious parade of its great works, it has made a silent, but indelible mark in the world. Its power has been in that great spiritual element so abundantly proclaimed, and through which alone, in its early days, it was enabled to promulgate so many and such important truths. In the science of government, Friends' views were so much in advance of all others, that they were persecuted and declared unfit to receive the favor of the king for uttering such sentiments. These were not idle words. In Rhode Island proper, separated from the Providence Plantations, where the governor and all the magistrates were Quakers, the most beautiful system of government that the world has ever seen was carried into effect. When war raged around, and fire and fagot and the tomahawk were doing their work, Rhode Island, sustained by the principles of equity and justice, remained uninjured. A still more striking instance occurred in the settlement of Carolina. That great philosopher John Locke, skilled in the learning of the world, who had written extensively on government, on toleration, and the rights of man, from his superior wisdom, was solicited to form a constitution for the new colony. The work was accomplished. It was the pride of its day. It was wise in the learning of books, and in the examples drawn from history. All its nice adjustments were of no avail, and the Carolinas found no settlement until a Quaker, John Archdale, of Buckinghamshire, was called to administer the government upon the Quaker principle. The world can furnish no stronger evidence of the power of the spiritual element, in contrast with the sensuous

theory, that man receives truth through the eyes
and the ears. Locke was a remarkable man, and
most of all remarkable because, upon philosophical
grounds, he denied altogether Friends' great idea
of spiritual intelligence in the mind. In Carolina
the two systems were brought in juxtaposition; the
one was a total failure, the other so remarkable
for its success, that the Quaker governor was publicly congratulated upon the event.

The governments of West Jersey, Delaware, and
Pennsylvania were in advance of the other colonies. Pennsylvania was the admiration of the
world. The philosophers and princes of Europe
were unsparing in their commendation of its principles. The British criminal code was so far re-
laxed, as to erase the penalty of death from one
hundred and fifty different offences. The ministry protested against such legislation, but the
colony maintained its ground in despite of severe
opposition. It was the Quakers of Pennsylvania
who first remonstrated against African slavery; it
was they, above all others, who extended the hand
of kindness and sympathy to the aborigines of the
country. The address of one of the chiefs to him
who had been the principal agent in this work of
humanity, is so simple and natural, as to be worthy
of preservation: it is in these words : " We called
at our old friend James Logan's. To our grief we
found him hid in the bushes. We pressed him and
prevailed with him to assist once more on our ac-

count at your councils. He is a wise man and a
fast friend to the Indians, and we desire when his
soul goes to God, that you may choose in his room
just such another person, of the same prudence and
ability, the same tender disposition and affection
for the Indians." Their exertions rested not in
public affairs. Wherever the rights of man were
invaded, there, in their early days, were the Quakers found ;* and though the Society itself may
have declined, confidence has increased from generation to generation in many of those testimonies
which were promulgated by the early Friends :
peace instead of war ; temperance and moderation ;
the disuse of oaths ; the devastating effects of a
paid ministry ; the elevation of the female sex,—
came first practically into operation in the Society
of Quakers.

Friends, without any improper self-exaltation,
may claim that they furnish no criminals for our
jails ; that a public pauper never was known among
them ; that the separation of the conjugal ties is
mostly if not altogether unknown ; that the cries
of wives and children abandoned are not heard
among them. The question may be asked, whether

* Both Charles II and James II, in the extremity of their
distress, placed themselves in the hands of the Quakers for
protection, and were not deceived. They carried Charles to
France, and refused all reward; and James was placed, through
their means, out of the reach of his enemies, and enabled to
reach Duncannon, after his reverses in Ireland.

the Discipline has been a means of producing this moral superiority. I answer, no. Laws to preserve order and regulate society are a necessary element of organization, but the power of reformation is not in them, but in the organic principle of Quakerism itself. If that is not the moving spring, all its testimonies are vain. Yet there can be no doubt that every society should retain the power to restrain abuses to which it might be subject; and a severe Discipline was unquestionably more needful in the early days of the Society, when enthusiasm and fanaticism seem to have taken possession of the British mind. But such laws are not needed now, and their existence is an incalculable injury to the Society. The exercise of this Discipline, by unnecessary disownments, has made divisions in families without number. It has made records of the feelings of one generation to be read by those who come after them, and to be a lasting stigma upon their character. It has done still greater injury to those "sanctified members," who have administered the Discipline. Men of natural kindness and benevolence in their private capacity, are made hard-hearted in the exercise of the Discipline. Men are injured by their own sins, and not by those of their fellow-men; and a steady perseverance in correcting evils; strengthening the feeble-minded and such as have no might of their own; and restoring those who have missed their way, would be more honorable, more consistent with Christianity, and probably give to religious minds more consolation, than anything that could be derived from the disownments that take place. There have been many who have separated themselves from the meetings of business because they would not be a party to these disownments. I have before quoted the words of Elizabeth Fry: I think she says in one place that she only seemed to go to meetings of business to witness the unkindness of the Society towards her children. It may be said, they had violated the Discipline. This only proves the truth of her expressed ideas, that Friends dwelt too much in the outward.

A reverence for the past, altogether inconsistent with the elementary principles of Friends, has kept this Discipline alive in its spirit, and almost to the letter, to the present day; and this, abused as it has been, and is ever likely to be under the present organization, has been one of the prominent causes of decline in the Society.

I have thus dwelt upon secondary causes, always however, persuaded that if the organization of the Society had been upon rational principles, and the power had rested with the people, there would have been no privileged classes, and these secondary causes would never have existed. I again quote from William Penn upon the subject of organization. He says: "The great end of all government is, to support power in reverence to the people, and to secure people from the abuse of

power." And when, in solving the controversy
respecting government, he says : " Any government
is free to the people under it, where the laws rule,
and the people are a party to those laws, and more
than this is tyranny, oligarchy, and confusion."—
(See Appendix to Proud's History of Pennsylvania.)
These were evidently general principles, which
were considered unchangeable. At the time they
were promulgated, William Penn was perpetual
governor of Pennsylvania, and Robert Barclay, of
New Jersey. In forming the civil codes for their
respective colonies, the rights of the people were
carefully protected, safeguards were provided
against the abuse of power, and the people were a
party to the formation of the laws, by which they
were to be governed. Robert Proud says of Pennsylvania : " That the enjoyment of that rational
freedom of thinking and religious worship, with
the just and equal participation of natural and
civil rights, has been both the cause and the means
of the unparalleled felicity, for which this Province
has been long so justly famed above all other
countries, at least in America, if not in the whole
world."—(See Proud's History of Pennsylvania.)
The same men who formed the civil code of these
colonies, Barclay and Penn, were prominent in
organizing the Society of Friends. They both
wrote extensively in favor of the Discipline, ne-
glected those safeguards which I have stated were
essential to every organization, and the result has

been schisms almost without number, disunion, and discord. Such are the truths of history, which cannot be evaded.

Had the civil code of the early colony of Pennsylvania been as contracted as that made by the same men for the Society of Friends; if they had placed the supreme authority in the hands of supposed sanctified individuals, curtailed the liberty of the press, infringed those civil rights which were guaranteed to all, by the Constitution of Great Britain, all of which was effected in the Society, Pennsylvania, instead of being the admiration of the world, would have been a reproach, and other parties would probably have been called in to administer the government on rational principles, as was done in Carolina. The compensation against these abuses of power, for I can call it no less, has been the excellent character of the individual members of the Society. For more than a century and a half, they have had to bear the weight of these contradictions. The struggle has been arduous and severe, and it is to some minds a matter of doubt, whether the Society is to be crushed by them, or has sufficient vitality to rise above them.

Let no one entertain the idea that there is an inherent decadence in the Society. To do so, would be to impair the ability to apply a remedy. There seems to be a natural tendency to association in the human mind, and unless we can believe

that man's spiritual nature will decay, we cannot
believe that the Society will decay.

It would not be too much to say, that in the
vital element of Quakerism, all men are Quakers.
As the Israelites are figuratively said to have
drank of that rock that followed them, so, with
equal truth, it may be said, that all men the world
over, Jew or Gentile, bond or free, are participants
of that spiritual element which is alike the foundation and superstructure, the alpha and omega, of
the Quaker faith. Some few there are whose
minds are so constituted as to suppose that the
Divine power is approached by many words, and
by the childish ostentation of popular Christianity;
yet it is not in the nature of things, that these pue-
rile forms should obliterate true Quakerism. This
is eternal and unchangeable, and can never be
done away. Those forms, and dogmas, and peculiarities, which have no vitality in them, will fall.
The struggle may be long and severe, but assuredly they will come to an end.

I write not thus to eulogize the Quakers,—such
an idea is foreign from my mind; but when the
most erroneous pretensions are made, that crime
and degradation are to be obliterated by means of
scholastic education ; when the pulpit is putting
forth its pretensions, that the world is to be reformed through its means, sometimes degraded by
a mercenary spirit,—I may be permitted to refer to

the silent operation of the spiritual element in man as being superior to them all.

I have endeavored to draw the line of distinction between this element, which is unquestionably the foundation-stone upon which the Society rests, and those forms and doctrines which have been suffered to overlay it and impair the manifestations of its beauty; and, I may be asked my opinion how a better state of things may be arrived at? The remedy is simple. Nothing abrupt is required. Let the members be restored to their individual rights; let the sense of the meeting still be the governing principle; but let that sense be decided not by the clerk, not by a few favored members, but by the voice of all, either personally or by representatives.

I know of no other means to avoid those abuses of power which have been so manifest in the Society. That portion of the Society called Hicksites have begun this excellent work. Let them encourage free discussion; let them open the press; let the Discipline be simplified; suffer the idea to prevail, that the principal objects of such a society is to restore, and not to cut off. That the weak, the feeble, the criminal, if such there be, have most need of the fostering care of the Society;—hence, let disownments cease, except perhaps in some peculiar cases.

Let the Society establish one point,—that order is to be preserved under all circumstances; that every organization requires a supreme power, and that in creating this, the voice of every individual should be heard ; that thus, all should be participators in making laws that are to govern all.

It may not be needful to pursue this subject further, seeing that a properly organized body should best know its wants. The great object to be attained is to restore to each individual the rights that properly belong to him as a member of Society. It is known, indeed, that each has a right to express his sentiments in the meetings for discipline, but it is a right that has little practical value with those who are not accustomed to public speaking, and who are scarcely permitted to utter sentiments of an ultra character.

Separated from their sectarianism, Friends are still a great people; and the greatest and perhaps the best among them are those who are most separated from narrow-mindedness, and from the complicated machinery of their organization. Many who are not members of the Society are the truest Quakers. This kind of Quakerism is increasing in the world, and probably will never decline, until (in the words before quoted) " The Egyptians be dead upon the sea-shore, and the raging sea is dried up."

I repeat what I have heretofore said, that there is not a society in the world that could dwell in peace with organic laws so contradictory. So long as effect will follow cause, the consequences are inevitable. If we desire peace, let us establish peaceable principles, and peace will as naturally flow therefrom, as the waters of a river or a brook into its accustomed channel.

In truth it may be said, as well in morals as in physics, that effects are inevitably combined in the causes from which they proceed.

Herein we have a certain guide to the means of resuscitating the Society, and giving it that strength which it has long needed.

That sympathetic feeling, so often an attribute of religious association, is grateful to many minds, yet we need not thence lose sight of this fact, that every organization among men is alike a civil compact, and that its successful development consists in the harmony of its parts.

A society dependent upon the affections of its members, should give to each that representation which is his due, and place the sovereignty of the society not in an oligarchy of uncertain appointment, but in the members themselves.

In a warning to the magistrates and inhabitants of Aberdeen, republished and sanctioned by the Society, there is this remarkable sentiment : "Oh consider, and say not in your hearts, as those atheists recorded in Scripture, 'All things continue as they were at the beginning, and where is the promise of his coming.'" In this short sentence, properly interpreted, we have at once, not only the cause of the decline, but the means of resuscitating the Society.

NOTE.

I have assumed, in this Essay, a decline in the Society of Friends, and such has been the case in Great Britain, where the prize was offered for the best essay on the subject; but there is no data by which to ascertain the fact as regards this country, and it is quite certain that it has not been here so distinctly manifested.

Each of the two divisions of Friends have held, in their usual course, their annual meetings on this continent; and in Philadelphia it has been estimated there have been in attendance from seven to eight thousand members. This indicates a large increase; but probably this increase will not compare with most other religious societies.

THE
NATURE OF WAR,

TOGETHER WITH

SOME OBSERVATIONS

ON THE

COERCIVE EXACTIONS

OF

RELIGIOUS SOCIETIES.

BY

WILLIAM LOGAN FISHER.

"Every battle of the warrior is with confused noise and garments rolled in
blood." ISAIAH ix. 5.

PUBLISHED FOR THE AUTHOR BY

T. ELLWOOD ZELL,

Nos. 17 and 19 South Sixth Street.

1862.

PREFACE.

The writer has endeavored to inculcate this interesting truth, that there is a harmony attainable in all moral affairs, conformable to the Divine Laws, and coresponding to the harmony of the universe; that it applies to all organizations among men, whether political or ecclesiastical; that in proportion as it prevails, the welfare and peace of man is promoted, and that every deviation from it is a seed of war.

The writer is quite sensible of the difficulties of demonstrating a subject which depends rather upon conviction than upon argument. He only sketches general principles, assuredly believed to be true, leaving it to younger minds to fill up the outlines.

Wakefield, 5th month, 1862.

THE NATURE OF WAR.

Active warfare is so barbarous in its character, so revolting in its details, as hardly to receive that careful analytic examination, to which a subject having so extensive an influence on society is justly entitled. Its causes should be traced, not with a view of supporting any theory, but by the philosophical mind in the hope that a knowledge of the subject would be one of the surest means of mitigating its horrors, and if that might be, of ultimately doing it away. The question has been often asked, whether war is consistent with Christianity? and almost as often answered in the negative. Until men clearly define what Christianity and war are, this question cannot be answered. As interpreted by one of the most intelligent Episcopal Clergymen in England : " The whole existing theology of Christendom, is based on the doctrine of original sin, and the doctrine of the atonement and vicarious sacrifice he states to be inseparably interwoven with it."* And war, as generally understood, is the resort to arms, or actual fighting.

* See Foxton on Popular Christianity, page 169.

1*

Yet each has a more exalted signification. Christianity, though bearing comparatively a modern name, we shall not greatly err in supposing, to be coeval with humanity. It is a principle of the mind, existing in its own power, and we degrade it when we make it dependent upon the accidents of time, all of which are subject to change. It appears to us to have no connection with original sin, with a vicarious atonement, or with any of those dogmas that are connected with the Christian name. These serve to amuse sectarian minds; they are prolific sources of private discord and public war. Though entertained with great sincerity, and as such deserving a certain degree of respect, they appear to have no real vitality in them.

Though Christianity received from Christ its name, we have abundant evidence to show, that his religion was spiritual, and had no dependence upon these things.

If peace is to be construed into non-resistance, then we may at once decide that war is in its whole character and bearing anti-christian. Yet it is evident that society is not at present prepared for non-resistance, and it would be as unwise as unjust, to exclude those from Christianity who believe it their duty to fight.

There are those to whom every precept in the New Testament becomes a law; these may find sufficient justification to resort to force in the demonstration made by Christ in clearing the temple at Jerusalem of the money changers, and of those who sold doves. It admits of a demonstration that self-defence is a principle that is implanted in all created beings. Where this should begin or end, must be left to the candid consideration of serious minds; and I refer to a subsequent page of this work, where I design to show that peace, established on a right basis, is always preferable to war.

War is defined by Vattel, in his work on the Law of Nations, as "that state in which we prosecute our rights by force." It is not only the act of war itself, or the manner of prosecuting it, but the principle of applying force for the preservation of human rights. The root of war, as defined by the best lexicographers, is not only the profession of arms or art of war, but " to strive, to struggle, to quarrel, to be in a state of opposition."

War, or the doctrine of force, exists in every possible degree, and throughout the world. It is often the work of despots and princes, for their own aggrandizement, and as such is entitled to unmitigated condemnation.

War is not necessarily an evil; it is the effect of causes which in the present state of society appear inevitable. Like the storm and the tempest in the natural world, its tendency is to purify, to renovate, not to destroy. If it is sometimes the work of despots, it is also the upheaving of nations for their own reformation. Anarchy is worse than war. It is better that a mob should be repressed by force, than that a government should be given up to its control. If war is, as often supposed, a scourge from Divine Providence, we may feel the assurance that it does not return void, but that it performs its mission, though man may not always be able to perceive its immediate effect.* It is the offspring of violations of the Divine harmony. The centre of this harmony is the mind of man, and it is not too much to say that all who violate it are accessaries to war. It is violated by individuals in their private capacities; it is violated by associations in arrangements which are contradictory in themselves, and which must in their nature produce discord.

All the arrangements of Divine providence from the sun, the centre of our system, to the smallest asteroid, from the ocean to the dew-drop, mark unerring harmony.

Even the physical economy of man, complicated as it appears to be, is yet in all its parts adapted to the end proposed. The smallest disarrangement produces as its necessary consequence, suffering. Every thing that we see, every reflection that we can make, points to analogies between moral and physical things; and

* Heeren's Historical Grecian Researches has the following: (page 246.)

The moral, like the physical world, owes its purification and its maintenance to the storms which sweep over it. But centuries and their generations must pass away before the operation of them is so fully developed as to allow the dim eye of human intelligence to embrace and give judgment upon the full extent of their results.

thus without being seers or prophets, we may predict with certainty events that are to follow from causes that are before our eyes : and we may hence feel assured that there is an appointed harmony as well for nations as for individuals ; as well for the moral affairs of men which move on the face of the earth, as for the planets in the heavens. Some of the most important discoveries that ever were made were the result of deductions having for their basis the assumed universal harmony of the Divine Laws; thus Columbus sought beyond the western skies for an equipoise to the eastern continent and the result was the discovery of America. The same course of reasoning led Lavoisier to suspect a deficiency in the equilibrium of the heavenly bodies, as established by the schools, and the planet Neptune was discovered ; it was in fact, proved that it must exist before it was found.

Facts of this nature are met with in every branch of physics. Science seeks for analogies, and relies with confidence on a harmonious correspondence with the Divine Laws, yet it is otherwise in the moral affairs of men ; philosophers erect systems without foundation, discordant in themselves, such as any intelligent child might be ashamed of; the result is, discord war and revolution, and they know not whence these come, nor where is the proper remedy.

It is learned ignorance of this kind that produces the popular doctrine heretofore referred to, that Christianity is founded on original sin. This and other dogmas equally absurd, being at variance with

the harmony of the universe, are every where the seed
of war.

The only true foundation for the moral affairs of
men is, the immediate revelation of God to the soul ;
it comes, we know not how, and at times when we
look not for it.

Dugald Stewart, one of the most eminent philosophers in Europe, referring to these "unintelligible
propositions," says that "they are liable to insur-
mountable objections, and have been adopted by in-
genious men, in preference to the simple and sublime
doctrine, which supposes the order of the universe to
be not only at first established, but every moment
maintained, by the incessant agency of one supreme
mind,—a doctrine, against which no objection can be
stated, but what is founded on prejudices resulting from
our own imperfections. This doctrine does not exclude the possibility of the Deity's acting occasionally
by subordinate agents or instruments.

Elsewhere, speaking of our moral sentiments, he
says, "They carry along with them the most evident
badges of this authority, which denotes that they were
set up within us to be the supreme arbiters of all our
actions, to superintend all our senses, passions and
appetites, and to judge how far each of them, was
either to be indulged or restrained. *

It is a reflection upon man, and much more so if
that were possible, upon Him who made him such, to
suppose that there is a natural tendency to evil in the

* Dugald Stewart's Works, vol. 3d, pp. 434, 442.

human character. On the contrary, the tendency is to virtue, not to vice; to good, and not to evil; to peace, and not to war. This assumed ascendency of virtue in the human mind is the foundation upon which the American Government rests ; if it be not so, then the system will prove a failure. It is probable that there is not an individual on the wide expanse of earth, who has not a preference for virtue instead of vice, for truth instead of falsehood; who would not prefer good to evil. We hear much said about the malign influence,—*evil* for the sake of *evil*,—it is a word which has no anti-type, and should be banished from our literature. Confidence in the mercy and justice of God will hardly admit of the belief that He has created a devil to torment us, or passions, in themselves evil, to betray us. Let us rather suppose that they are all good in themselves, and that it is the abuse of them that is wrong.

The first and highest duty of man is to take care of himself; yet an undue regard to self is the curse of our day, and it is this that is the cause of war ; let this be brought to an equilibrium, and wars would cease.*

* Whatever theologians may choose to assert, it is certain that mankind at large has far more virtue than vice, and that in every country, good actions are more frequent than bad ones. Indeed, if this were otherwise, the preponderance of evil would long since have destroyed the human race, and not even have left a single man to lament the degeneracy of his species.—*Buckle on Civilization, Vol. 1st., page* 109.

Wm. Penn's *Holy Experiment* was founded upon this great idea, that man is a recipient of the revelation of God in his own soul, by which, being enabled to govern himself as an individual, he was equally competent as a member of a community, and as a citizen of a State.

Such an experiment, if it had been attempted either in Massachusetts or Virginia, would have been a failure. Men act naturally under the instincts implanted by their antecedents. A free government with them had no foundation to rest upon. The laws of those colonies did all they could to destroy those elements from which a free government would naturally come, and yet these elements have been proved to be true. It is from this source that the United States derive all their power.

The smallest worm that crawls on the earth is guided to its proper destination by the revelation of God. We may call it nature, or instinct, or innate ideas, or what we please, it must at last be resolved into a harmonious co-operation with the Divine laws, according to its state. On this revelation applied to man, rests not only government, but the whole fabric of human society,. A careful examination of the records of history will demonstrate one unchangeable truth, that every deviation from this harmony leads to discord. This is the lesson that politicians ought first to learn in conducting the affairs of men. There may be no certain protection against evils produced by designing men, but assuredly there

is a protection against those wars that are the result
of contradictions in the organic laws or usages of societies or nations. Let intelligent men be convinced,
that these contradictions are inevitable in their results, and as far as they are desirous of promoting
peace, so far will a remedy be found. A benign
Creator has not made man to struggle unceasingly
with evils resulting from these contradictions, without
appointing a remedy. That remedy has been but
partially applied by the present arrangements of society. Much has been left undone that is within the
power of man to accomplish. There is a natural recuperative power in man; and if in the individual,
then also in society; if in the physical frame, then also
in the mental constitution. Thus it is that the tendency of evil is to cure itself; man defeats even this
by interfering with the laws of Divine Providence.
If we admit that war is inevitable in the present state
of society, which I do not admit, its evils may be ame-
liorated in various ways.

A very extended scheme for mitigating its horrors was
proposed by Henry IV. of France, in the year 1610.
It was communicated to Elizabeth, Queen of England,
and, after her death, to James. The hand of Ravaillac,
which destroyed Henry, put an end to this scheme.
Though it might have been in many of its details chi-
merical, yet there can be no doubt, that international
legislation upon the subject of war, entered into by
two or three of the larger powers of Europe, would
have an important influence in doing away with some

of its most revolting features. All private property and private persons might be, by agreement, protected. To prevent the dangerous exercise of private war, and to settle the disputes of individuals, the sovereign power, in all civilized countries has established statute law, with officers to execute its provisions, whose ulterior resort, in all cases, is the sword. Thus, the statute, or civil law, is a modification of war; and thus, also, are the local laws of individual societies; or, if the term is preferred, they are all alike modifications of peace, their whole scope and object being this:—to preserve peace and good will among men. Without these provisions, it will be readily perceived that society would be dissolved, and become a mass of inconceivable confusion.

A profession of peace changes in no respect those laws which exist in their own nature, and by which nations are governed. Let us not deceive ourselves. No organized society can be non-resistant; the very compacts by which they exist are founded on war. They pre-suppose the ability and the intention to sustain themselves.

Within a few years several members of the Society of Friends, among the most peaceable of all societies, have been incarcerated in the prison, in Philadelphia, at the suit of other members as peaceable as themselves, respecting the common right to a cemetery. Force, also, is applied as required, for the preservation of that decorum in their meetings which is indispensable to every organization. Thus demonstrating

what has been already observed, that the profession
of peace, changes not those laws, which, being impera-
tive, supersede all local enactments, however refined
and excellent they may appear to be.

The attempt was made in Pennsylvania, at its first
settlement by the Quakers, to establish the government upon peaceable principles, without the use of
the sword. So far as being preserved from actual
hostilities, it was remarkable for its success, and this,
in itself, was great gain. While other colonies were
carrying on desperate conflicts with the Indians, Pennsylvania remained at peace; but, if peace is to be construed into non-resistance, it was a failure. It was
not long after the government of William Penn was
established before the courts were engaged in trials for
piracy; thus demonstrating the necessity of force, in
carrying on a peaceable Quaker colony. Even before
this period, an attempt to tax Quaker emigrants coming
into the Delaware was agreed to be resisted, as being
unconstitutional. At the head of these resistants was
a Quaker preacher, by the name of Jennings. The
remonstrance upon this subject is preserved in Smith's
History of New Jersey, and, so far as it appears, this
paper, written, as it is stated, by William Penn, on
behalf of a colony of which Robert Barclay was Governor, was the first protest against taxation without
representation, which came from this continent, and
which was the principal cause of the American Revolution.

Can any serious mind doubt that these things were

all right ? Sincere and intelligent minds, in their day, were carrying on a quasi war, consistent with the situation in which they were placed, having for its end the promotion of peace.

I shall place at the end of these pages a letter from James Logan, explaining his difficulties in his attempt to carry on a peaceable government, in the early colony of Pennsylvania. This letter, forwarded to the Yearly Meeting by his son, William Logan, was referred to a Committee of Samuel Preston and others, who reported " that the subject matter related to the civil and military affairs of the government, and, in their opinion, it was unfit to be read in the meeting." It was stated that the letter came from one who was known to have had abundance of experience, was an old member, and had a sincere affection for the welfare of the Society. These remonstrances were vain; the letter was rejected. Those who are familiar with our early colonial history will, probably, assign to James Logan the most important position in the province, after that of William Penn. For many years almost the whole direction of public affairs rested with him. Gordon, in his history, states that, though, in some cases others held the name, yet the power rested with Logan; hence it is that his opinions are entitled to especial consideration. He had a difficult path to tread; he was expected to preserve peace, with a people not prepared for peace. On the other hand, there were powerful Indian tribes, whom it was not very difficult to conciliate; but there were thousands of bigotted sectarians, who came to this country, carrying the Bible in one hand and the sword in the other, declaring that the saints were to inherit the earth, and the heathen to be exterminated. They took possession of some of the best land in the province, to the estimated amount of one hundred thousand acres, setting all law at defiance.*

Thus were sections of Pennsylvania controlled for many years by lawless fanatics, perhaps of all others the most dangerous men, and the most difficult to govern. The obvious course would have been to have suppressed them by military force, and in one sense the Friends who objected to this, might be considered responsible for the consequences. These fanatics seemed to believe that it was their duty to murder the Indians, and in revenge the Indians carried off the white men women and children, and there was no power to control them. These things culminated in their breaking into the gaol at Lancaster, and murdering a number of friendly Indians who had taken refuge there. Three hundred of them came as far as Germantown on their way to Philadelphia, to commit the like outrage. The Quakers and others to the number of one thousand took up arms, and before this superior force, these worse than savage white men retired; thus demonstrating the necessity of military power in preserving the peace among lawless men, even in a peaceful community. William Logan and Edward

* Watson's Annals.

2*

Pennington, two eminent Quakers, were the most conspicuous in defence of the Indians.

The Edinburg Review, has said "that if Princes would use Friends for prime ministers universal peace would be perpetuated." This is true to a certain extent, but there are two other things requisite; first, that there should be a peaceable population; second, that the civil organization should be harmonious; neither of these requisites existed in their completeness in Pennsylvania. There were contradictions in the colonial government, arising principally from the attempt to combine the assumed rights of a propriactory government, with a popular assembly. James Logan's services were invaluable, and much was accomplished. Yet the wantonness of lawless men appeared to him to require, coercive measures; and in a letter to Franklin, dated several years after the foregoing to the Yearly Meeting, he used these words, " ever since I have had the power of thinking, I have clearly seen that government without arms is an inconsistency." (See Franklin's works, vol. 7, pp. 25.)

Logan was dead when these poor Indians who had sought the protection of the government were murdered. The history of the transaction demonstrates the correctness of his views. This evidence which admits of no doubt, evinces that the attempt to enforce principles on minds not prepared to receive them, instead of being productive of good, is productive of evil.

What Logan endeavored to accomplish in a regular way, without unnecessary violence was finally

brought about by irregular warfare; and there can
be no reasonable doubt that war in this case was a
blessing, as putting an end to a reign of terror, alarm-
ing to the peaceable inhabitants without any guarantee for the future. During the early part of the
French Revolution, the Friends who were settled in
France,* asked of the French National Assembly to
be released from military duty. Mirabeau, the Presi-
dent, the most eloquent man in Europe, made this
reply :—

"Quakers who have fled from persecutors and
tyrants, cannot but address with confidence those
legislators who have, for the first time in France, made
the rights of mankind the basis of law. And France,
now reformed, France in the bosom of peace (which
she will always consider herself bound to revere, and
which she wishes to all other nations) may become
another happy Pennsylvania.

" You say that your religious tenets forbid you to
take up arms, or to kill on any pretence whatsoever.
It is certainly a noble philosophical principle which
thus does a kind of homage to humanity. But consider well, whether the defence of yourselves and your
equals be not also a religious duty ; you would otherwise be overpowered by tyrants. The Assembly will,
in its wisdom, consider all your requests, but whenever I meet a Quaker I shall say, ' My brother, if thou
hast a right to be free, thou hast a right to prevent

* The principal man in this deputation was the elder Wm.
Rotch, of New Bedford, Mass.

any one from making thee a slave; as thou lovest thy fellow-creature, suffer not a tyrant to destroy him; it would be killing him thyself. Thou desirest peace; but consider, weakness invites war.' "

Had Mirabeau known the real facts, instead of admitting that the Friends of Pennsylvania were peaceable men, he would probably have said, that they were warriors who had unwisely laid the train for the destruction of those poor defenceless Indians, who had a right to claim their protection.

The world, with all its vast extent, and varied nations, presents few fields so accurate, so full of interesting data, connected with the welfare of man, as this country, from its colonial beginning to its combined power as a nation, and to its present civil war.

The colonies were embryo empires, sufficiently large to demonstrate the truth and value of particular principles and doctrines, and yet so small that their re sults may be clearly ascertained. The history of the American Colonies is full of instruction, but it is written in vain if we attend not to its teachings. All the different forms of government known to the British Constitution were carried into effect in these colonies.

In considering the subject, let us bear in mind, that every organization, be its name or character what it may, civil or religious, is subject to the same general laws. It is an error to suppose that there is more sanctity in what is called a religious than a civil compact; the one may be to the other as a wheel within a wheel; their spheres may be different, but those general principles that are right in one, are equally essential to the other; what is wrong in one is wrong in the other; wherever true harmony exists among men, there is religion, let it bear what name it may.

I quote on this subject the sentiment of that individual, whose opinions have had more influence than those of any other, for the last two hundred years. Lord Bacon, respecting the Church of England, asks this question, " Why the civil State should be purged and restored by good and wholesome laws, and the ecclesiastical state should continue on the dregs of time without alteration ?" And he adds :—" I could never find but that God had left like liberty to the church government that he had done to the civil government." See Bacon's Works, Philada. Edition, page 421, 422.

Thus it is that the history of civil governments may furnish important lessons to religious organizations, if they are willing to be instructed thereby. The first emigrants to this country were of a superior class of men. They came here avowedly to establish their favorite doctrine; they enacted their own laws, and it is for us to mark the issue, and to derive from it all the instruction it conveys. As a class, they were what was termed religious men, many of them, no doubt, of unquestionable piety. Some of the colonies were settled by Roman Catholics, others by different sects of Puritans, Brownists, Baptists, &c. The Quakers settled the little island of Rhode Island, West Jersey, Pennsylvania, Delaware, and Carolina. They appear before us in two aspects. As civilians they were in advance of all that the world had yet seen, and it is to them that this country is indebted, for those true conceptions of the rights of man which have been so much admired. In forming their religious organizations, they were perhaps behind all others. Principles which they rejected as civilians, they embraced with ardor in their ecclesiastical government. The civil laws of Pennsylvania enacted by the Quakers made the press free, their ecclesiastical laws placed it under a severe censorship. Many of the most important civil rights were granted to the early colonists by William Penn, while the same men rejected them in their religious organizations. After pleading most earnestly in England for liberty of conscience, they seem, like the Puritans of Boston, when they came to this country, to have forgotten those great principles of liberty for which they had so manfully contended in Europe. With this difference, that while in Boston, they incorporated their narrow-minded sectarianism into the civil laws, the Quakers confined their exactions to the members of their own society.

Let us carefully mark the result. These civil laws have been copied again and again as new States were added to this Confederacy, and they now form often in the original words of Penn, the elementary basis of the laws of important and extensive communities. Thus, so far as we can judge, they will remain a monument to his memory, more enduring than brass or marble, while the power of those ecclesiastical laws

which he contributed to establish, has gone forever.
A more impressive lesson could hardly be furnished.
In the one case the laws were made to conform to the
great principles of human nature, which were readily
acknowledged by all men throughout the world ; in
the other, they were narrowed down to the color of a
ribbon, or the cut of a garment. The result was certain. It was foretold by wise men, who saw its absurdity. Narrow-minded sectarianism can never be
received as truth by any intelligent society, and the
time will assuredly come when all this petty supersti-
tion, all this idolatry to forms will pass away, or such
as retain it will be buried in its ruins.

The early governments of this country, beyond the
Quaker settlements, exhibit few marks of intelligence.
Each of these colonies endeavored, according to its
views, to establish peace as the best means of promoting its prosperity. In every case there was a failure. Those measures which promised peace, even-
tuated in discord, and in many cases in actual warfare; for this obvious reason, that there were continued
encroachments upon what appeared to be the inherent
rights of man, and the result was discord.

The proprietors of Carolina asked the celebrated
John Locke, to form a system which might promise
peace and prosperity. It was even a greater failure
than the rest, and was scarcely more than formed before it was abandoned.

To William Coddington, of Rhode Island, a man
who came to Boston as an Episcopalian, and being

banished thence for his religious opinions, found shelter in the little island of Rhode Island, belongs the high honor, of having first proclaimed on this continent the true principles of civil liberty. There was in his little colony a complete separation of Church and State. There were no civil laws of coercion upon religious subjects; even a Sunday law, which made a distinction between days, while rigidly enforced in the adjoining colonies, was not enacted in Rhode Island. Massachusetts and Virginia, each attempted systems of coercive religious creeds which produced unnumbered difficulties. The Providence plantations, and Maryland, established systems of uncertain toleration. In the one, Papists were not allowed to enter the colony; in the other, the penalty for denying any of the three persons of the Holy Trinity, was death.

This fact is certain, that when by the adoption of the Federal Constitution, and the operation of local causes, the contradictions of the individual colonies came to an end, then for the first time there was tranquillity.

We may learn from these historic facts, the insufficiency of all laws to preserve and protect religion. In every case history proves them to have been false, and, according to our theory, if false in a state or colony, they are equally false in a religious organization. Such laws existed in every colony excepting those settled by Friends. The whole power of the government was enlisted for their support; their repeal was violently opposed on the ground that it would be the destruction of all religion. It was accomplished; and instead of injury, to the manifest advantage of society. Among Friends, the evil was confined to their own religious sect. The evil was less extensive, but the principle was the same. Those who are convinced that religion is altogether voluntary, might readily believe that it was not promoted by coercive enactments.

In most of the American colonies, ecclesiastical and civil affairs were so closely blended, that it was not easy to decide which had the greater power. One fact admits of no dispute, whether these laws were ecclesiastical or secular, they were utterly worthless to accomplish the end proposed, which was the improvement of the moral and religious condition of the people. In addition to this, they were barriers to all true civilization, to any just comprehension of the rights of man, and of that civil liberty which is essential to the well-being of every society. The Society of Friends, which I have stated, settled several colonies, confined their severe ecclesiastical laws to the members of their own religious association, and among them these evils have been most manifest, producing those schisms, wars, and revolutions which have disgraced the Society, and will continue to disgrace it so long as they exist, and they will continue to exist so long as the causes remain. No profession of peace, however refined it may be, will save them from this result. With these historic facts before us, may we

not judge from analogy, as well as from those eternal
principles that are always open before us, that the repeal of every ecclesiastical law of a coercive character,
and the abrogation in religious societies of all those
childish dogmas to which I have referred, (leaving
them to be judged of by individuals without reproach,)
might be an important means of preserving peace?
Friends attribute these schisms to disorderly persons,
to fanatics, and the like. This is not the case. The
real difficulty is in the contradictory elements of the
organization. These are like swords put into the
hands of unscrupulous men, to accomplish ends which
the wise and good had left undone.

These are universal principles applicable to all
times, and all people.

An eminent British statesman, travelling in France
before the Revolution, thus writes:—"All the symp-
toms which I have ever met with in history, previous to great changes and revolutions in government, now exist and daily increase in France."*

These causes finally produced the most memorable
revolution on record. A clear perception of the tendency of those measures, which, by impairing the civil
rights of the people, were gradually undermining and
destroying the government itself, is not so remarkable
as the fact, that they are not always foreseen and
guarded against. In accomplishing this revolution,
the fish-women of Paris, and the dregs of society, if I
may use such a term, acted an important part. The

* Chesterfield's Letters, Dec. 25th, 1753.

reason is this : they had been crushed and ground to
the earth by a long series of oppressions, and as was
the tension, so was the rebound.

It was a revolution more thorough and severe than
ever had occurred in Great Britain, for this obvious
reason : the flexible nature of the British constitution
admitted of continued amelioration and improvement.

I have referred to the American colonies because
their history is at all times within our reach, and the
deductions from facts admit of the strictest examination ; yet the elementary principles, carried into effect
therein, are peculiar to no nation or age of the world.
Great Britain and France, in the same climate, in-
habited after the conquest by people of the same
origin, manifest on a larger scale, all those principles,
which have been referred to in the sketch I have
given of the American colonies. Great Britain owes
that freedom for which it has been conspicuous, and its
comparative exemption from severe internal convul-
sions, to a steady regard to the rights of all its people.
The same equal justice that was meted out to the
rich, was meted out to the poor. William the Con-
queror, crushed with one blow all arbitrary distinctions; there was one law, for the poor and for the
rich. The Saxons rebelled, but the Normans, who
were conquerors, crushed them with their power; this
has been the corner stone upon which the superiority
of Great Britain still exists.* Every revolution, from
that time to the present, now eighty years, has re-

* De Lolme on the English Constitution, page 16.

sulted in increased regard to the rights of the masses.
The people claimed, from King John, the great Charter, which, for the first time in the annals of the
world, gave the right of property to slaves, securing
to them their toils. Whenever the rights of the people were infringed, then trouble began. In every
contest the oppression was defeated, and human rights
enlarged. Many people look to Great Britain as the
exemplification of the best government in the world;
whatever it is, it has been made such, by yielding to
the laws of Divine Providence, in the elementary
principles of its constitution. When the government
did not yield to the wants of society, the people took
the affairs of the nation into their own hands, and
accomplished their own ends, in their own way. The
nation was saved from internal revolution during the
latter part of the last century, by the determined pur-
pose of the "Pot-house politicians," Wilkes, Church-
hill, Temple, and others, who, probably, from no good
motive, made use of the cry of "liberty" to accomplish those changes, to which her best men, reposing
at their ease in the enjoyment of their wealth, were
too well satisfied with things as they were, to consent.*
The Monarch was not safe; the government was
afraid to carry into effect its own edicts. It yielded,
and was saved.

These pages are too limited to attempt more than a
very hasty review of those important events, which
have had so marked an influence on the welfare of

* Horace Walpole's George III, vol. 1, p. 182.

succeeding generations. It may be sufficient simply
to refer to the difference between Great Britain and
and France. In Great Britain, as I have stated, the
rights of the people were always paramount; in France
there were superior classes of men, who were first to
be provided for. The great laws of Divine Providence were disregarded; the nobles and clergy came
first, and this is the uniform distinction between those
principles which govern the two nations. The result
is before us. The two nations were, as I have stated,
originally settled by the same people, and a man
must be blind, indeed, to the facts of history not to
perceive their effects; on the one hand, civil liberty,
with all it attendant blessings; on the other, supersti-
tion, with all its curses. Not only in Great Britain
and France, but in all the states of continental Europe, Spain, Denmark, Sweden, &c., wherever history
reaches, the truth of these great principles is exem-
plified, and they tend to demonstrate the possibility
of forming organizations, of what kind soever, civil
or religious, that will produce peace, as their necessary
consequence, instead of war.

The ingenuity of man has been able to form ma-
chines, to a great degree perfect, to accomplish his
various ends in life. He can detect any jar which
impedes their progress. Why should he not, also,
form a government, harmonious in all its ways, which
should, in its nature, produce peace, and not war?
Government is a machine, formed by the hands of
man, and within his control. Assuredly, wherever

there is discord in a civil or religious society, there are contradictions, which admit of a remedy. This subject is all important to the peace and welfare of society, and should be carefully considered by the wisest and best among us.

There are some remarkable facts tending to demonstrate the truth of these views. Although the early Colony of Pennsylvania was by no means perfect in its peace, yet there is great instruction in considering how much was attained, and the causes by which its more perfect development was impaired; so much was done as to demonstrate that much more might be accomplished; and it is a fact that admits of no dispute, that in those parts of Pennsylvania, where the Quakers have still retained their influence, the offences against the laws have, for a long series of years, greatly diminished. Were our history more perfect, we should, probably, find abundant confirmation of the correctness of our reasoning.

Basil Hall found, at the Luchoo Islands, to the South of Japan, a people of very remarkable honesty and integrity; and these people he states to be without any means of defence, and utterly ignorant of the art of war.

In the midst of Southern Italy there is an independent republic called San Marino. It proudly stands from time immemorial, uninjured, in the midst of a country desolated by wars; the prototype of a civil association, the most perfect and admirable, such, as before it was formed, existed only in the Utopias of Philosophers. (See Irvin's Letter, American Review.)

At the Northern extremity of Europe in Norway, there is a district called Stavanger, with forty thousand inhabitants. I give the words of a traveller respecting their prison. "Their prison is kept by an old woman, she had but one prisoner in it, and had so much confidence in him that the door of his cell was kept open."

A Judge after twenty-five years experience gave this account, "The average number of crimnals has been from six to seven a year, mostly on account of small thefts."

If these are facts, applied to one people, they are not partial in their nature, but applicable to all. .

CONSTITUTION OF THE UNITED STATES.

With few exceptions the Constitution of the United States is a harmonious compact. These exceptions have been fatal to its peace. Had the framers of the Constitution been wise enough in their generation, clearly to have foreseen the inevitable nature of the contradictions of that instrument, and firm enough to have resisted them, we should have been saved from the present civil war.

Almost with one accord in and out of Congress, slavery has been considered the immediate cause of the present rebellion. It is unquestionably the remote cause. Without slavery, we should have had no war. But the immediate cause is not slavery, but the Constitution, and we should reserve our censure for the framers of that instrument. It was they who introduced contradictions into that compact, the result of which was discord.

The country had publicly asserted the equality of man; yet the framers of the Constitution denied this, by establishing a superior order of men, essentially a class of nobility, with guaranteed rights founded on human bondage, which gave them the control of the government. When, from the force of circumstances, this came to an end, they rebelled. This, and not slavery, is the cause of the present war.

If the slaves were in rebellion, the case would be different; then slavery would be the immediate cause of the rebellion. Instead of acting as a first part, the slaves are acting at best but a secondary part: comparatively they are inert.

It is the favored few, the politicians, who have had great gifts bestowed upon them, and who like the horse leech, are still asking for more; more gifts and more power; it is they alone who are making all the present disturbance, and it is not too much to say, that until they are conquered and crushed out we shall have no peace in the country.

The contradictions in the constitution of the United States were wholly unnecessary. Our government is of a mixed nature with two sovereign powers; yet unhappily, to a limited extent, it has made itself a party to slavery. First, in consenting to hold a territory wherein slavery was a component part. Second, by the rendition of fugitive slaves. Third and chiefly, by granting

peculiar privileges in the councils of the nation to the
owners of slaves. These are the causes of the present
war; and whatever settlement of the question may
hereafter be made, they ought never to be continued.

Let the Slave States draw what cordon they please
around their own property, to protect their slaves, but
let the territory that is now free, be free forever. This
should be the law of the land. Let the southern slaveholders adopt one of two courses, let them make
their slaves men, or relinquish forever the idea of their
being represented in the national councils. In addition let all the Territory of the United States be free.

With these principles we need not be afraid of any
new compact. It would be harmonious, and as such
necessarily peaceful.

I have thus considered slavery purely in its political aspects; I see no evidence of a rising among the
slaves, nor that the country is ripe for emancipation.
On the contrary, and it is a great unhappiness that
it should be so, State after State is rising up to prevent the introduction of fugitives into its territory.

The slaves are learning from the air they breathe,
and the circumstances which surround them, and from
those benign influences of Divine Providence, to which
allusion has been made; and the time may probably
come, even if the power of slavery is confined to the
individual states, when the slaves will assert their
rights; when revolt and revolution, and desperate
conflicts may arise from the slaves themselves asking

to be restored to their long lost liberty. The prevention of this is in the hands of the slaveholders themselves, in yielding to the slaves, from time to time, at least a portion of their just rights.

If there is any truth in the scope of my remarks, it is to this effect: that there is a recuperative power in moral as in physical affairs, never inactive, but in accordance with its nature, educing good out of evil; and that every attempt to force results out of their proper course is more likely to produce evil than good.

There are benevolent men, and wild fanatics, often with the best intentions, who have undertaken to instruct the slaveholders what they ought to do, and what to leave undone. In general, these men are ignorant of what they write about, and often make statements which are not correct. They tell us that slavery is already ripe for extinction. This may be so, and the sooner it comes the better, because there can be no doubt that it is a foul blot upon the escutcheon of the country. But intemperate zeal, upon this or any other subject, is productive of harm. Whenever slavery is done away, it must be by an act in which the slaves are participants; it is, at least, doubtful whether emancipation can be either promoted or retarded by the exertions of those who really have no connection with it. Slavery is, undoubtedly, silently working its own way to its final extinction, and, perhaps, the longer it is delayed, the more certain and effectual it will be.

The case is a very plain one—amelioration or war. But, if the United States, as a government, is clear, we shall, necessarily, be clear of the consequences.

In the correspondence between John Adams and Thomas Jefferson, they often expressed astonishment at the harmonious working of the American Government. They were wise men in their way, but they were men of authority, tinctured with the doctrines of the universal depravity of man, without seeming to have a conception that there was an unchangeable basis for moral as well as for physical affairs; a power existing in itself, which, being safe for individuals, was the proper guide for nations; that the people, left to themselves, are disposed to good rather than to evil. A government formed upon this basis is, necessarily, the strongest government in the world; its foundation is the principle of peace, which is always stronger than the sword. These eminent men, great as they were, appeared to have no conception of this great truth.

When the proprietors of Carolina asked John Locke, perhaps the most eminent philosopher of Europe, to form a Constitution, they had confidence in him, because he had the experience of the world before him, yet he committed the like mistake. He was a man of authority, and he failed, and the work was accomplished by an humble individual, who attended to the instincts of nature, which are the Divine laws.

Most persons familiar with history will recollect the extraordinary facts connected with the formation of the Justinian Code; men of authority, familiar with the learning of the East, were employed to accomplish it; so perfect was it believed to be, that the penalty of death was made the punishment for every attempt to change it, yet it was a failure, for the same reason that destroyed Locke's Constitution of Carolina. While these eminently wise men were drawing their precedents from all countries, society moved quietly onwards, and left them with their precepts and laws adapted to former generations, but unfit for the present.

It may be absolutely necessary in the present state of society to be guided by precedents ; but, while the world moves onward, they are stationary, and thus inadequate to meet the wants of the day. It is precedents enlightened by common sense; authority, with enlightened reason to guide it, which is valuable for man. And yet religious societies, as they are called, seem proud of the precepts they have obtained from their forefathers, and the professed teachers, instead of being guides to instruct, are left behind to grope their way in the dark, and to learn from those whom they profess to teach.

Truth is not the offspring of authority in things of an intellectual nature, and hence the failure; it is the revelation of God alone, that can properly adapt means to ends. In proportion as men deviate from these great principles, they destroy that equilibrium which is needful for the harmony of moral affairs, and

lay the foundation for strife and contention in society,
and war and bloodshed in nations.

It may be doubted whether any of the larger religious societies are free from contention and strife.
Such societies are social in their character, and appear to meet the wants of certain portions of the community; but, if man can give religion to his fellow-
man, then may he erect ladders, and climb to Heaven,
in his own way. Religion is individual in its character, and cannot be transmittted from man to man.

"The world by wisdom knows not God."

The Quaker elder, George Fox, said, that though
he read of Christ and God, he knew them not, but by
the like spirit in his own soul. This is a great and
interesting truth. There is a duality in man's ideas ;
all outward things are known by outward means ; but
purely intellectual ideas are received only by intuitive
perception, innate ideas, or by whatever else we may
call the intellectual power. Thus by the mercy of
God, all men upon the subject of religion are placed
upon a footing; we may teach sectarianism in all its
debasing forms ; we may teach the social and moral
duties of life in all their beautiful proportions, man
may perhaps direct his fellow man to those sources of
truth whence true harmony comes, but religion is, so
far as we can judge, the communion of God with the soul
of man, and has no necessary connection with the teachings of men. We are quite safe in saying, make the
systems of society harmonious in themselves, and

there will be little need of the sword. Within the last few weeks, several remarkable papers have been issued by the Friends in Philadelphia. They are remarkable, as coming from a society making above most others the highest professions of peace.

It is not within the scope of these pages critically to examine these works. The best course seems to be to let them quietly pass into that oblivion which is their proper destiny. These papers, under the disguised form of preserving their ancient testimonies, breathe forth the very spirit of war. Yet they are put forth by men excellent in their way, who have reasoned correctly upon false premises, and thus their whole argument falls to the ground. Friends make, perhaps, the highest profession of religion of any organized body, while at the same time they are perhaps of all others most severe, and as a natural consequence most contentious.

I may properly, in pleading the cause of the Quaker soldier, which I design to do, and in exemplifying my general position, note some interesting facts respecting the ancient history of Friends.

Coleridge, in his " Table Talk," uses this language: " It is amusing to see the modern Quakers appealing now to history, for a confirmation of their tenets and discipline, and by so doing, in effect abandoning the strong-hold of their founders. As an "imperium in imperio," I think the original Qnakerism a conception worthy of Lycurgus."

For more than a hundred and fifty years Friends have denied any change in their views; they might as well attempt to reconcile light with darkness. The early Friends, unhappily, had not confidence in their own convictions, and they fell under the debasing influence of authority. They, whom no prisons appalled, who yielded to no cruelty, even unto death, were not strong enough to maintain their own simple views when assailed by that debasing influence of sectarian bigotry, by which they were surrounded. Disputes almost without number occurred, and Quakerism was changed from the endeavor to establish the dominion of truth in the soul, to a kind of gladiatorial contest, for the establishment of particular doctrines, of the truth of which, both themselves and their opponents were equally ignorant.

As a consequence, instead of peace, there were schisms without number, contentions and public disputations, or more properly revolutions, having precisely the same source as those revolutions to which I have referred in the history of nations. They did not originate with the people, but in the rulers, who impaired the inherent rights of man. They were contests without bloodshed, war according to the fashion of Friends, all that the state would permit them to practice. The facts admit of no dispute, and their melancholy effects are witnessed to the present day. It ought never to be said that Friends are a peaceable society; they cannot be peaceable, whilst carrying into effect a system of contradictions.

If Friends desire that schisms should continue to occur, that there should be unkindness instead of brotherly love, let them pursue the arbitrary measures which have been marked out; let them disown the members, who, during the present contest, have taken up the sword, and those who pay military taxes; or let them learn the important lessons which history teaches; that peace was restored to the adjoining colonies of New England and Virginia, whenever they ceased to interfere with the private rights of individuals.

Assuredly, if the Society of Friends proceeds to exercise its discipline, and after making great professions that men should be guided by their individual sense of duty, disown those who have endeavored to restore peace to the country by the sword, there will be another schism. It can only appear grossly inconsistent to ask the members to make an apology for an act which they performed from no selfish motive, but from their own sense of truth.

PRINCIPLES OF PEACE.

An examination of the principles of war need not argue any disrespect to that more elevated state of society in which war could have no existence. It may be accepted as an unchangeable truth, that without deviation from that harmony which is essential to the perfect happiness of man there could be no war.

Peace may, in some respects, be considered the opposite to war, yet it is not a negative, but a positive principle, existing in individual minds, the strength of which no man has yet fathomed; it is the conservative principle of the world, and wherever it is manifested, there is strength in proportion thereto.

The beautiful Jewish song, on the subject of peace, need not be lost sight of, though the Society may not realize it.

"Thou wilt keep him in perfect peace whose mind is stayed on Thee, because he trusteth in Thee;"* but not more impressive than the expressions of James Naylor, the Quaker martyr, published and approved by the Society:—"There is a spirit that I feel, that delights to do no evil, nor to revenge any wrong; as it bears no evil in itself, so it conceives none in thought to any other; its crown is meekness, its life is everlasting love unfeigned, and takes its kingdom with entreaty, and not with contention, and keeps it with lowliness of mind." †

These sentiments of Naylor, published, at length, in the Quaker books, and forming part of their creed, have probably not their equal, for beauty and strength of ideas, in the whole catalogue of theological literature. They sustain the sublime idea that to the purified mind there is no evil. George Fox had previously said in, perhaps, the deepest sentiment he

* Isaiah xxvi. 3.
† See Sewell's History, article Naylor.

ever uttered, "That, though he read of Christ and God, he knew them only from a like spirit in his own soul."

The address of William Leddra to his friends, before his execution, breathes, also, the sublime spirit of perfect peace:—"My spirit is as if it did not inhabit a tabernacle of clay, but is wholly swallowed up in the bosom of eternity, from whence it had its being."

The spirit of peace breathed forth in these beautiful extracts has no necessary connection with religious societies. It extends to all nations and societies throughout the world, and it is always a blessing wherever found—nay, further, there is a protection in it, which the world knoweth not of. Every individual has partaken of it, the world over, and by its power alone, men have been able to decide that peace is preferable to war. Men can only testify of what they know. It is by the power of this spirit, operating in the hearts of our fellow men, that we can safely travel from place to place, or walk by the way side.

What then, is to be done, when narrow-minded men attempt to deny to Friends that civil liberty, which seems to be the inherent right of all? I answer this by the following opinion of George Fox: When, on his visit to America, he was at Providence, Rhode Island; finding there a law abridging the rights of the people, he addressed them, thus:—"You are the unworthiest men on earth, if you do lose the liberty in which Christ has made you free in life and glory."

In other words, assert your rights.—See *Bancroft's History*, vol. 2, page 68.

The object, with religious societies should be to reform, not to cut off. We often hear, in the recommendation in Friends' Meeting, that we should "return to first principles." Now, I seriously ask, what is the first principle in the Society of Friends? If I am not greatly deceived, it is this: that each individual should endeavor to understand his duty, by calmly considering the convictions of his own soul; and, knowing them, that he should practice them with simplicity of heart. This is, unquestionably, the only true principle on which the Society of Friends rests. Notwithstanding that this is seriously promulgated, from week to week, and from year to year, I ask, whether it is really believed in? whether the pleadings of these conscientious men, who, having joined the army, under the purest convictions of duty, or of those who are about to pay military taxes, are to be regarded or to be set at naught?

It is a self-evident truth, that absolute personal liberty is inconsistent with government of any kind, and this applies as perfectly to religious as to civil society. *That* is not liberty, but licentiousness, which impairs the equal rights of others; herein is a clearly defined line, where restraint begins and liberty ends. Another principle, equally, though not so well understood, is this: that government shall leave individuals, as much as possible, to govern themselves, and never unnecessarily interfere with their private rights. On those two foundations both civil and religious society may be safely built.

The Society of Friends, in its original organization, was remarkable for the most simple and beautiful creed, or elementary principles, that ever engaged the attention of man. It was not Christianity or Quakerism, limited to a sect, but that broad philosophy of eternal wisdom, which embraced all true men, whatever their particular local distinctions might be. Thus, Edward Burroughs, one of the most eminent of the early Friends, says: "Abraham and Isaac, and Moses, Habakuk, Daniel and Paul, and all the rest were Quakers, though they were not so in name." Again, " David, Moses, Jeremiah, with many more testified of in the Scriptures, were of the same faith with us ; and the same doctrines, principles and practices, for themselves, were Quakers, as their own writings manifest." (Folio Works, page 322 and 165.)

Such sentiments manifest an interesting truth, that primitive Quakerism overlooked minor differences, when men were supposed to be true to the great principle of religious duty. Some of those men were eminent warriors. Why should they be approved, and acknowledged to be Quakers, and the warriors of the present day rejected? If I mistake not, the doctrine of Burroughs is true Quakerism, or, in another word, true Christianity; it is that which has affinity with the wise and good of all ages, nations and people.

An essential ingredient to these enlarged views was not wanting in ancient Quakerism. Francis Howgill, in his testimony concerning Burroughs, uses this language:—"When it pleased the Lord to raise up to us the ancient horn of salvation, we met together, in the unity of the Spirit, and the bond of peace, treading down under our feet, all reasoning, questioning, debating and contending about religion, or any part or parts, or practice or practices thereof, as to any external thing; and mightily did the word of God grow among us." *

Now I would seriously ask whether these Friends who are contending under the names of Orthodox, Hicksites, Gurneyites, Wilburites, &c., are really Quakers, according to ancient Quakerism which they profess to reverence? I think not, but rather that they are warriors armed at all points, to contend, to oppose, to quarrel. And yet these are the men who are foremost in disowning those, who do not conform to their own narrow-mindedness.

The time probably is not distant when it will be deemed as improper, to make the dogmas of Christianity essential to a religious, as to a civil organization. They may be interesting to particular classes of individuals, but from the least to the greatest, they have no vitality in th·m, and may be as safely banished from religious, as from political creeds. Those who are now contending about these affairs may be Quakers according to the modern acceptation of the term, but if so, then has Quakerism sunk into an abyss of

* See Introduction to Edward Burroughs' Works.

sectarianism, and is really of no value. Penn and Barclay, men of great classical learning, quote the sentiments of hundreds of the most eminent Greeks and Romans, to show a correspondence of sentiment and feeling with Quakerism as they understood it. Penn's "No Cross, no Crown," almost his first work, was replete with these extracts.

I attach no authority to the extracts from Friend's writings. There are many beautiful sentiments in them, but when they descended to sectarianism, they lost their power and uttered contradictions, which have been productive of great evil.

It is an idle pretence that they have not changed their creed or elementary principles. Grant men these premises, and they can prove logically whatever they desire. For nearly two hundred years, they have by publications without number, been endeavoring to conform their doctrines to popular Christianity.

Every limitation of these broad philosophical truths is sectarianism, injurious to every society, and degrading to the character of man.

It was in an exhuberance of feeling that Burroughs exclaims, " My confidence is sure that the work of the Lord shall prosper, and our testimony shall be glorious forever, and this people shall never be extinguished from being a people." See Folio Works, page 767. This prophecy is fulfilled in the present day; such Quakerism as this will never die. It is not the transient ebullition of a couple of centuries, but will live forever. It is the narrow-minded secta-

rianism that passes under the name of Quakerism
that is in danger, and it must come to an end.

The strength of man the world over is in the spiritual element. Of all ancient nations, the Grecians
were the most spiritually minded, and comparatively
they excelled in everything, and the superiority which
is justly due to the Society of Friends for their elevated views of civil government, is to be attributed,
not to the learning of schools, but to the internal convictions of their own minds. When they attempted to establish their principles by arguments, then
their power departed; in less than fifty years
there were three important schisms, and they have
continued with more or less frequency to the present
time. The members engaged in these schisms were
excellent in their private capacities, their individual
character was beyond reproach, yet the causes existed, and the effect was inevitable, and thus it will
be in time to come. The more the attempt be made
to carry into effect the contradictions of the discipline,
the more schisms, and weakness, and decline will be the
necessary consequence. The effect cannot be changed;
it is inevitable in the nature of things.

The sentiments of Burroughs on the subject of war,
appear to have been adopted and sanctioned by the
Society of Friends. As rational and intelligent men,
they of course appreciate peace, but they fully ac-
knowledge in many instances, the necessity and pro-
priety of war. The articles upon the subject are too
lenghty to be copied into this essay, but they are

clear and explicit on the subject. It was nearly a hundred years after the Society was organized before there was any discipline for disowning soldiers, and it is very evident that little regard even at that time was paid to it.

Several of the early Friends addressed the army, among whom were George Fox, Samuel Fisher, and Edward Burroughs. See the addresses of the latter in his works. The whole purport and spirit of these addresses is this: not that they should lay down their arms—nothing of that kind is said—but, that, they shall be faithful to their calling; telling them that the Lord had a great work for them to do, in going to Rome and demanding of the Pope that he should give up his torture houses and Inquisitions, and assuage the blood of the guiltless, through all the dominion of the Pope. Burroughs says:—"The Lord hath owned and honored our English army, and done good things for them, and by them, in these nations, in our days;" and he exorts them "to be faithful, that they may do the Lord's work, in avenging the blood of the innocent."

Isaac Pennington, one of the early Friends, thus writes:—"The present state of things may, and doth require the use of the sword; and great blessings will attend the sword, where it is borne uprightly to that end, and its use will be honorable."—*Pennington's Works*, folio, page 323.

Barclay says:—"The magistrates have not come to the pure dispensation of the Gospel, and, therefore,

while they are in that condition, we shall not say that
war, undertaken on a just occasion, is altogether unlawful for them." (See *Barclay's Works*, folio,
page 537.) And, so far as I can judge their writings,
this appears to have been the general feeling among
the early Friends. (See *Thomas Story*, folio journal,
page 621.) George Fox's doctrinals. (See index.)

There is a curious address of George Fox to the
council officers, preserved in some of the controversial
writings of the day, and which I presume to be au-
thentic, though not found in his works, in which he
proposes to the army, to go to Rome and demand of the
Pope himself, that all his torture houses, and racks,
and inquisitions, should be given up, and he intimates
that many Quaker soldiers have been put out of the
army by their faithfulness to the Lord in saying, *thou*
to a single person, and wearing their hats. The address is too long to be inserted here, but it explicitly
recognises the beneficial uses of the sword.

William Penn's sentiments upon war are unmistaka-
bly exhibited in his "Essay toward the present and
future peace of Europe." He proposes an alliance
of the European powers for the promotion of peace,
so strong that all would be obliged to submit ; his
words are these, " If any of the sovereignties that
constitute these Imperial States shall refuse to submit their claim or pretensions to them or to abide
and perform the judgments thereof, and seek the
remedy by arms, all other sovereignties united as one
strength shall compel the submission and perform-

3

ance of the sentence with damages to the suffering party," &c.

A more complete system of defensive war could hardly be formed. It was not original with Penn, but had been adopted and enlarged by him, with all the particulars needful, as he supposed, to its execution. The grand Seignor of Turkey was to be compelled to submit, under the threat of the loss of his territory in Europe. Not satisfied with this, two years after, in the year 1697, Penn proposed to bind the British North American Colonies together, " to consider the ways and means to support the union and safety of these provinces against the public enemies." Both these papers, containing the same ideas, evidently came from the same mind. A copy of the latter may be found in an address of Edward Armstrong, before the Historical Society of Pennsylvania. In addition to this, I may refer to the fact, that upon two occasions Penn applied to the Legislature of the colony to comply with the Queen's request, to appropriate money for the defence of the frontiers.

It may not be needful to advert to those rights of a military character which were contained in the charter from the Crown granting to Penn the province of Pennsylvania, further than to say that he was invested with power to levy and muster all sorts of men, to make war, and to pursue his enemies as well by sea as land, and by God's assistance to vanquish and take them. Without these powers he would not, in its proper sense, have been sovereign of the territory, and the necessity of his accepting it, serves to show the inconsistency of two professions which must necessarily clash with each other.

None of these sentiments are conclusive, but whilst the authority of the early Quakers is deemed so paramount, it cannot be thought irreverent to refer to them, and it may be assumed that they are more in accordance with common sense than the modern innovations.

The present war is not a common contest, it is one by which the nation is seeking to preserve a compact which is deemed essential for the good of the whole ; it is an effort to preserve peace, of like character with that of Friends, when they resort to physical force for the preservation of their rights. Many of the Quaker soldiers are as true-hearted men as are to be found. They are not habited in Quaker dress, use no peculiar language, yet many of them are performing the first Quaker obligation, in endeavoring to do what they believe to be their duty. This is in accordance with the doctrine of the Society, inculcated from day to day, and from year to year. What can they do more ? But for this they are condemned, not because they have done wrong, but because it is written in the Quaker law, that men may not fight.

Finally, all may agree, that peace is preferable to war; but let us bear in mind that war is preferable to anarchy, and that it is better to enforce obedience to the laws by the sword, than to deliver up nations to disorderly men. This is consistent with common sense, (the most valuable of all sense,) with enlightened reasoning, the most valuable of all the powers of the mind.

Grievous and desolating as this war is, inflicting on individuals, as its necessary consequence, deep and abiding sorrow in sundering the dearest and tenderest ties of life; yet may we not hope, that in its consequences under a beneficent and wise Providence, it may yet produce to our country, blessings that it has never known before. One thing is manifest already; the distinctions that have heretofore separated us are in a degree broken down; we are now one nation, seeking with one heart and one mind the restoration of harmony. Happy indeed it will be if this should increase, and the nation find itself united in common brotherhood for the happiness of all. Then indeed the cause of war in this nation would in a great measure be ended.

A LETTER FROM JAMES LOGAN

To the Society of Friends on the subject of their opposition in the Legislature to all measures for the defence of the Colony.

MY FRIENDS,—It is with no small uneasiness that I find myself concerned to apply thus to this Meeting; but as I have been longer and more deeply engaged in affairs of government, and, I believe I may safely say, have considered the nature of it more closely than any man besides in this province; as I have also from my infancy been educated in the way that I have ever since walked in, and I hope without blemish to the profession; I conceive and hope you will think I have a right to lay before you the heavy pressure of mind that some late transactions in this small government of ours has given me; through an apprehension that not only the reputation of Friends as a people, but our liberties and privileges in general, may be deeply affected by them.

On this head I think fit to mention in the first place, that when, above two and forty years since, our late Proprietor proposed to me at Bristol to come over with him as his Secretary, after I had agreeably to his advice taken time to consider of it, which I did very closely before I engaged; I had no scruple to accept of that, or any other post I have since held; being sensible that as Government is absolutely necessary among mankind, so, though all Government, as

I had clearly seen long before, is founded on force, there must be some proper persons to administer it. I was therefore the more surprised when I found my master on a particular occasion in our voyage hither, though coming over to exercise the powers of it in his own person, here showed his sentiments otherwise :* but as I have ever endeavoured to think and act consistently myself, observing that Friends had laid it down as a principle that bearing of arms even for self defence is unlawful, being of a different opinion in this respect though I ever condemned offensive war; I therefore in a great measure declined that due attendance on their meetings of business that I might otherwise have given.

I must here nevertheless add further, that I propose not in offering this to advance arguments in support of the lawfulness of self-defence, which amongst those who for conscience sake continue in a condition to put strictly in practice the precepts of our Saviour, would be altogether needless, but wherever there is a private property and measures taken to increase it by amassing wealth according to our practice, to a degree that may tempt others to invade it, it has always appeared to me to be full as justifiable to use means to defend it when got, as to acquire it.

*This particular occasion was the meeting of a supposed privateer on the passage, when Logan prepared to fight in order to assist in defending the ship, while William Penn retired below. The particulars of this transaction will be found in Franklin's works, being an account received from Logan himself. It is added that William Penn appeared pleased with the conduct of his Secretary, who told him that if he had commanded it, he should have retired with him.

55

Notwithstanding which I am sensible our friends
have so openly and repeatedly professed their principles on that head to the Government, and they have
thereupon been so much distinguished by their favors
as a peaceable people from whom no plots or machina-
tions of any kind are to be feared, that I shall consider this as I have said to be their standing and
avowed principle, and only offer to your consideration what I conceive to be a clear demonstration, that
all civil Government as well as military is founded on
force, and therefore, that Friends, as such, in the
strictness of their principles, ought in no manner to
engage in it: as also, that as we are a subordinate
Government, and therefore, accountable to a Superior
one for our conduct, it is expected by that Superior
that this Province as well as all the other British
Colonies shall make the best defence against a foreign
enemy in its power, as it was required to do by the
late Queen Anne in the last French war, upon which
the then Governor raised a militia of three com-
panies of volunteers, but for want of a law for its
support, it dropt in about two years after, and the like
orders may undoubtedly be expected again, when
another war with France breaks out, which is said now
to appear unavoidable. That is of the greater importance to Britian, as it is for other reasons most
assuredly to ourselves, that the country should be de-
fended, as it is in the heart of the other British Colonies. It is well known in Europe that from the vast
conflux of people into it from Germany and Ireland,

numbers who can bear arms are not wanting for a defence were there a law for it, as there is in all the other British Colonies I think without an exception.

That all Government is founded on force, and ours as well as others, will be indisputably evident from this : King Charles II., in his grant of this province to our Proprietor, directed that the laws of England for the descent of land and the preservation of the peace should continue the same, "until altered by the legislative authority;" and our government continues on the same plan, with Judges, Justices, Sheriffs, Clerks, Coroners, Juries, &c. all of whom who act by commissions, have them from the Governor in the English form. The English law is pleaded in all our Courts, and practitioners copy as near as they can after the practice in Westminster Hall.

By that law, when the peace is commanded even by a constable, all obedience to that command manifestly arises from a sense in the person or persons commanded that resistance would be punished, and therefore they chose to avoid it ; but in civil cases of more importance, the Sheriff who is the principal acting officer executes the judgments of the Court upon those they were given against which they are obliged to comply with how much soever against their will; for here also they know resistance would be in vain, or if they attempt any, the Sheriff is obliged by the law without any manner of excuse to find a sufficient force, if it be had in his county to compel to a compliance.

And in the pleas of the Crown, besides that he is

obliged to put to death such criminals as by the law have been condemned to it. He as general conservator of the peace, is likewise invested by the same law with proper powers for suppressing all tumults, riots, insurrections, and rebellions, on whatsoever occasion they may arise as far as the posse or whole force of his county may enable him; and for this end he receives, together with his commission, the Kings Writ of Assistance, requiring all persons within his district to be aiding him in these and all other cases, by which if need be they may freely use firearms and all manner of destructive weapons, and are not at all accountable by the law for any lives they may take in the opposition, any more than a man is on the highroad for killing another who attempts rob him; and such as refuse to assist the sheriff are by the same law liable to fine and imprisonment, from whence it is evident there is no difference in the last resort between civil and military government, and that the distinction that some effect to make between the lawfulness of the one and the other is altogether groundless. As none are killed in the field, so none are punished with their goodwill; a superior force is employed in the one case as well as in the other, and the only difference that I have ever been able to discover in their essentials is, that the Sheriff being but one person in the county, cannot possibly assemble any very great number together in any regular method or order, as in case of any insurrection in the city of Philadelphia would soon appear; but on the contrary in a regular militia, every man knows his commanding officer and whither to repair on a proper call. And from these premises it certainly follows that whoever can find freedom in himself to join in Assembly for making laws, as particularly for holding of courts, is so far concerned in self-defence and makes himself essentially as obnoxious to censure as those who directly vote for it.

Further it is alleged, that King Charles II. very well knew our Proprietor's principles when he granted him the powers of Government contained in the Charter; to which it is answered, that among the other powers granted to the Proprietor and his Deputies, he is created Captain General with ample powers to levy war against any nation or people not in amity with the Crown of England, which in case he were not free to do by himself, he might by his Deputies; and if he is invested with power to make an invasive war, much more is it to be expected, that he should defend his country against all invaders, and I am a witness that in those two years, or somewhat less, that the Proprietor took the administration on himself, when last here, he found himself so much embarrassed between the indispensable duties of Government on the one hand, and his profession on the other, that he was determined, if he had stayed, to act by deputy.

It is further alleged by our Friends, that no other was expected than that this should be a colony of Quakers, and it is so reputed to this day; that they are willing themselves to rely on the sole protection of Divine providence, and others who would not do the

same should have kept out of it, for nobody called or
invited them. But it is answered to this, that the
King's Charter gives free leave to all his subjects without distinction to repair to the country and settle in
it ; and more particularly the Proprietor's own invita-
tion was general and without exception, and by the
laws he had passed himself, no country, no profession
whatever, provided they owned a God, were to be ex-
cluded.

It is true our Friends at first made a large majority,
yet they are said now to make, upon a moderate
computation, not above a third of the inhabitants.
That although they allege they cannot for conscience'
sake bear arms, as being contrary to the peaceable
doctrine of Jesus Christ (whose own disciples, nevertheless, are known to have carried weapons), yet,
without regard to others of Christ's precepts, full as
express against laying up treasure in this world and
not caring for to-morrow, they are as intent as any
others whatever in amassing riches, the great bait
and temptation to our enemies to come and plunder
the place, in which Friends would be very far from
being the only sufferers, for their neighbors must
equally partake with them, who therefore by all means
desire a law for a militia, in a regular manner, to
defend themselves and the country as they have in
the other colonies.

In the last French war, Pennsylvania was but an
inconsiderable colony, but now by its extended com-
merce it has acquired a very great reputation, and

particularly that Philadelphia has the name of a rich
city, is known to have no manner of fortification,
and is as has been said a tempting bait by water from
the sea, and by land the whole country lies exposed to
the French, with whom a war is daily expected.

That the French in their last war with England
were so greatly distressed in Europe by a current of
yearly losses that they were glad to sit quiet where
they might, but now it is much otherwise, as they
appear rather in a condition to give laws to their
neighbors. That our Indians unhappily retiring west-
ward, have opened a ready road and communication
between this Province and Canada, by their settling
at Allegheny, a branch of that great river Mississippi,
which branch, extending a thousand miles from its
month where it enters the said river, reaches even
into this province, and between its waters and the
western branches of the Susquehanna there is but a
small land carriage. That the French exceedingly
want such a country as this to supply their islands
with provisions, and our rivers for an easier inlet into
that vast country of Louisiana which they possess on
the Mississippi than they now have by the barred
mouth of it, that empties itself a great way within
the shoal bay of Mexico, and they have many large
nations of Indians in alliance with them to facilitate
their conquests : for all which reasons our numerous
back inhabitants, as well as others, ought to be
obliged to furnish themselves with arms, and to be
disciplined as in other colonies, for their own proper

defence, which would be no manner of charge to the public and but little to particulars.

These I think are the principal arguments adduced by those who plead for self-defence, to which I shall add these other weighty considerations that may more particularly affect Friends as a people.

The Government, and particularly the Parliament of Britain, appear to have this war very much at heart, in which they spare no charge in fitting out large fleets with land forces, and expect that all their colonies will, in the same manner, exert themselves, as the Assemblies of all the others have in some measure done, ours excepted, not only in their contributions, but they have also generally a regular militia for their defence. Our friends have recommended themselves to the government, not only by their peaceable deportment, as has been already observed, but by complying with its demands in cheerfully contributing by the payment of their taxes towards every war. Yet they are admitted into no offices of the government, above those of the respective parishes where they live, except that some have undertaken to receive the public money; and though tolerated in their opinions as they interfere not with the administration, yet these opinions are so far from being approved by the Government, that when they shall be urged as a negative to putting so valuable a country as this, and situated as has been mentioned, in a proper posture of defence, those who plead their privileges for such a negative, may undoubtedly expect to be divested of them, either by act of Parliament, or a *quo warranto* from the King against their charter, for it will be counted equal to betraying it. And this, besides the irreparable loss to ourselves, must prove a reproach and vast disadvantage to the profession everywhere.

'Tis alleged the Governor made a false step last year in encouraging or suffering our servants to enlist, for which he has been abridged by the Assembly of the salary for a year and a half, that had for many years before been allowed to our Governors. But as this is interpreted by the Ministry as a proof of his extraordinary zeal for the King's service, his conduct herein, as also his letter to the Board of Trade, however displeasing to us, will undoubtedly recommend him the more to the regard of our superiors, in whose power we are, and accordingly we may expect to hear of it.

Our Province is now rent into parties, and in a most unchristian manner divided. Love and Charity, the grand characteristics of the Christian religion, are in a great measure banished from amongst the people, and contention too generally prevails.* But for the

---

*The contentions here referred to, have been so fully explained in the foregoing pages, as to make further reference to them unnecessary. The States of this Confederacy formed upon the principle of non-interference with individual rights, furnish the most conclusive evidence that government based upon right principles involves no necessity for contention. It is not assumed that these governments are perfect, but it is assumed that by a proper representation they are adapted to the wants of the

weighty reasons that have been mentioned in this paper, it is not to be doubted but that those who are for a law for defence, if the war continues and the country be not ruined before, must in time obtain it.

It is therefore proposed to the serious and most weighty consideration of this meeting, whether it may not at this time be advisable that all such, who for conscience sake cannot join in any law for self-defence, should not only decline standing candidates at the ensuing election of Representatives themselves, but also advise all others who are equally scrupulous to do the same. And as animosities and faction have of late greatly prevailed amongst us, and at all times there prevails with too many an ill-judged, parsimonious disposition, who for no other reason than to save their money, though probably on some other pretence, may vote for such as they may think, by their opposition to the governor, may most effectually answer that end.

That such Friends should give out publicly beforehand, when they find they are named, that they will by no means stand or serve though chosen; and accordingly, that the Meeting recommend this to the Deputies from the several Monthly or Quarterly Meetings in this Province.

All which, from the sincerest zeal for the public good, peace of the country, and not only the reputa-

people, and this is the secret by which the contentions of religious societies will eventually come to an end. When the people make their own laws there is nothing further for them to claim.

tion, but the most solid interest of Friends as a people, is (I say again) most seriously recommended to your consideration by

> Your true friend and well wisher,
>
> JAMES LOGAN.

Stenton, Sept. 22*d,* 1741.

To Robert Jordan and others, the Friends of the Yearly Meetings for Business, now convened in Philadelphia.